I0161438

Secret Messages in the Church

By
Jan Voerman

TEACH Services, Inc.
P U B L I S H I N G
www.TEACHServices.com ● (800) 367-1844

Copyright © 2013 TEACH Services, Inc.
ISBN-13: 978-1-4796-0177-6 (Paperback)
ISBN-13: 978-1-4796-0178-3 (ePub)
ISBN-13: 978-1-4796-0179-0 (Kindle/Mobi)
Library of Congress Control Number: 2013946119

Published by

TEACH Services, Inc.
P U B L I S H I N G

www.TEACHServices.com ● (800) 367-1844

Table of Contents

Introduction

There are few issues that cause more discussion in the church than the topic of Contemporary Christian music (CCM). The dialogue connected with this subject is usually very emotional.

Two important arguments for the use of modern Christian music in the church are, the desire to be progressive and up-to-date in order to reach non-church members, and the desire to keep our own youth and teenagers in the church.

An important question to ask in this context is what exactly is the purpose and meaning of the church service? Is it a moment of gratifying one's self or are we to glorify and praise God? Should we worship and praise our Creator with human preferences or should He only be worshiped according to divine principles?

Those who are for and those who are against modern music in the church, typically defend their arguments passionately. Unfortunately, the discussion frequently brings both parties into a contending and divisive position. However, the right and adequate information is not always at hand for a true and well-balanced opinion about the role and influence of music to be made.

Secret Messages in the Church is a good guide to help the reader form a just and responsible biblical view about the many different kinds of music. The book shows that popular music styles, such as rock and New Age, can be successfully used by occult powers to influence an individual's thinking and to obtain control over the human mind.

Secret Messages in the Church is primarily written for professing Christians who accept the Bible as the normative standard for their lives and who desire to follow seriously and obediently in the footsteps of Christ.

May the Holy Spirit grant the reader a clear insight while reading this book. May God bless the reader and provide the power to overcome and break with modern music styles that endanger a dedicated spiritual life.

Chapter 1

Deciphering the Secret

When countries are at war with each other, often messages of great importance and of a sensitive nature are sent. If the enemy were to intercept any of those secret messages he would gain a great advantage from them. Therefore, they are put into a secret code that only the recipient knows how to decipher. Thus, they become secret messages. If the enemy knows how to decipher them, much can be gained.

There are good and bad messages. Here is an example of a good secret message: *HCRUHC OT OG*. Can you decipher it? In this case, it is wise to comply with this message. It can influence your life in a positive way if you make it a regular habit. However, first you will have to decipher it before you can have any benefit from it. It may seem rather difficult, but the solution is quite easy. If you understand that the Hebrew language reads from right to left, you can apply that principle to this message, and the secret will be revealed.

When read backwards it says: Go to church. That is a good thing to practice regularly. But why did I present such a backward secret message? Just to amuse you in some way? No. In spiritual warfare we can be easily confronted, rather innocently, with crafty secret messages we ought to shun. These prevailing and far reaching messages are dangerous and we should not allow them to influence us in any way. But unfortunately, only a few realize their true nature and wide, penetrating influence.

In order to understand the aspects that are involved, such as the scope and character of the secret messages described and considered in this book, it is important to first have a clear picture of the great controversy between light and darkness that is raging in this world— the deadly struggle between Christ and Satan, which concerns everyone. We must determine whose side we will choose.

Chapter 2

Lucifer's Rebellion

In order to get a better picture of Satan's purposes and motives, which underlie all of his misleading activities, we should consider some characteristics of his life story.

Satan is a real being. He was created by God perfectly as a glorious and mighty angel of light, honored by the heavenly hosts. He was Lucifer, the heavenly Lightbearer. At a certain point in time however, he changed. He became gradually evil, and iniquity was found in him. The prophet Ezekiel writes, "Thou wast perfect in thy ways from the day that thou wast created, till iniquity was found in thee."[1]

How was it ever possible that iniquity was found in this once perfect being? It is a question that rings throughout all the ages. God is the Creator. He determines the boundaries of a happy life, filled with true, selfless, radiant love. The apostle Paul stresses precisely what these boundaries are for all of His creatures. The apostle explained, "For in him we live, and move, and have our being."[2] All His creatures, in all that they are, do, and plan, are to trust in Him as the Source of their lives, if they want to enjoy real peace and happiness and secure an everlasting bright future.

"God is love,"[3] and He embedded His unselfish, radiant love in all of His created beings. When these flames of love are kept within God's appointed boundaries, there will be an excellent atmosphere of delightful warmth. It is like the flames of fire that are kept burning in

1   Ezek. 28:15
2   Acts 17:28
3   1 John 4:8

a fireplace, producing comfortable warmth for everyone present in the room.

However, when the flames go beyond the boundaries and leap out of the furnace into the room, they will serve another purpose, not intended, and will soon become destructive. If these flames are not stayed; the whole house may be consumed.

Unfortunately Lucifer moved little by little beyond God's appointed boundaries by acting on his own, apart from His Creator. The flames of love leapt out to serve another purpose of self-exaltation. Instead of remaining a crystal clear, unselfishly loving creature, he gradually became a self-centered, murky, and mysterious destructive being. He did not stay in his Creator, in Whom he was to live, move, and have his being. The tragic outcome of this independent move was self-destruction and the ruin of all those who are deceived into following him.

Lucifer turned against his Creator. He wanted to walk on his own appointed, unlimited path of freedom, and he desired God's power. He kindled love for himself and declared, "I will be like the most High."[4] He aspired to authority and honor above his Creator. The prophet Isaiah tells us that he said in his heart, "I will exalt my throne above the stars of God."[5] Love for self, coupled with feelings of envious pride and haughtiness, eventually made Lucifer, in his megalomania request that he be honored and worshiped, instead of the Creator.

However, the difference between the Creator and the creation can never be taken away. God is the eternal Source of all living creatures. So Lucifer, in all of his wisdom and excellency, existed in complete dependence upon God as the only eternal Source of his whole being. A created being can never become independent from his Creator. When the angel of light wanted to exalt himself in the power of his unchecked and ever rising feelings of pride; he placed his feet on the dark path of self-destruction.

---

4   Isa. 14:14
5   Isa. 14:13

Thus, in Lucifer a new element of unlimited self-exaltation rose up, totally independent from his Creator. As a completely new and unknown plant, Lucifer's strange and unusual activities began to develop and grow in the perfect heavenly garden of God's creation. Would this new phenomenon be a valuable acquisition? Would it grow into a beautiful and graceful plant as Lucifer pretended it would become and one that many of the angels at his side accepted as truth? Or would it grow up to be a very dangerous and deadly poisonous plant, as the Creator, "Declaring the end from the beginning,"[6] knew beforehand?

If the all-wise Creator, knowing the devastating results of this sin of rebellion, would have uprooted and destroyed this plant right away when it surfaced, it would have raised doubt and uncertainty, and even worse still, an unhealthy fear of God, since the angelic hosts would not have been able to understand and foresee the results. Would the Creator be correct, or would Lucifer, the angel of light be correct? Lucifer, with much zeal and as a great benefactor, went about propagating this new, unknown phenomenon in an attractive way. He promised freedom, happiness, and independence from God to all created beings. Was he right? Many angels chose to follow him.

The only way to see where all this would lead would be to allow the plant to grow to full maturity, "Ye shall know them by their fruits."[7] This was the only way to unmask the real nature of this pretentious heavenly being and solve the problem of sin for all eternity in a definite and convincing way.

The angels who chose to follow Lucifer would never have imagined that this lovely angel of light would bring forth "evil fruit"[8] and harm any of God's created beings. They had no idea he would plunge the first human beings, Adam and Eve, into misery and death. They could never have thought that this "anointed cherub"[9] would instigate so much

---

6   Isa. 46:10
7   Matt. 7:16
8   Matt. 7:17
9   Ezek. 28:14

hatred against the dearly beloved Son of God, that one day He would be tortured and nailed to the cross. They could never have dreamed that this splendid being, covered with, "every precious stone"[10] would be the cause of millions of sincere Christians being persecuted, tortured, and burned at the stake throughout human history.[11] They never could have believed that this glorious; "son of the morning"[12] would go about, "as a roaring lion ... seeking whom he may devour."[13]

Feelings, plans, and ideas that are not quite in harmony with the Creator may at the outset look good and desirable and may even gain much support, because the deviation from God's order is at first often hardly perceptible. It is like a little lion cub that is so attractive, harmless, and touching when young, but that will someday grow up to become a dangerous, devouring beast of prey.

Lucifer has deceived himself and many others. At first it was almost imperceptible that his independent moves were contrary to God's rules. When God confronted him about the dead-end road he was following, he refused to humble himself with repentance, or to rectify his mistake. Feelings of shame and pride are often too strong to allow one to admit that a wrong choice has been made. The inevitable result will then be blind persistence in sin, enmity against God, and a continuance in darkness and deception. Such was the great controversy that started in heaven, which disputed God's rules and righteousness, and thus jeopardized the whole universe.

The Bible says that, "there was war in heaven."[14] Lucifer, once the angel of light, had become Satan, the enemy of God in heaven. He fought with his angels against God and His righteous government.

The angelic host was put to the test. Every angel had to make a choice to side with either the Creator or with Satan. The outcome of

---

10   Ezek. 28:13
11   Compare Heb. 11:34–38
12   Isa. 14:12
13   1 Peter 5:8
14   Rev. 12:7

the heavenly battle was the loss of Satan and his angels place in heaven, and he, "was cast out into the earth, and his angels were cast out with him."[15] Now the Earth became the great battlefield between good and evil.

Satan succeeded in getting the first human beings, Adam and Eve, on his side. As he had done in heaven, he suggested to them that the boundaries and rules that were set up by the Creator were a hindrance to real freedom and an obstacle in the path to attaining a higher sphere of living and progress.

Satan disputed God's command, and objected to God's declaration that Eve would die if she was disobedient and ate from the fruit of the forbidden tree. He insinuated to Eve that God kept her deliberately ignorant of true knowledge. He pretended that God was withholding from her the ultimate purpose of becoming gods.

The Bible says, "And the serpent said unto the woman, 'Ye shall not surely die: For God doth know that in the day ye eat thereof, then your eyes shall be opened, and ye shall be as gods, knowing good and evil."[16]

The result of Eve's submission to the misleading and lying words of Satan was the fall of man. Death entered this world through Satan, the prince and deceiver of this world.

However, there is hope. The happy news of the Gospel of Jesus Christ is that He partook of human flesh and blood, "that through death he might destroy him that had the power of death, that is the, devil; And deliver them who through fear of death were all their lifetime subject to bondage."[17]

Satan, the devil, is a conquered enemy. Christ through His death defeated him and provided the way of life for all who were and are subject to bondage. God loved the world so much that He gave His only Son, "that whosoever believeth in him should not perish, but have

---

15   Rev. 12:9
16   Gen. 3:4, 5
17   Heb. 2:14, 15

everlasting life."[18]

Praise God for this wonderful deliverance from the deceptive and destructive power of Satan. We can learn from Satan's rebellious life story some important features about his deceptive power.

1. He undermines the Creator's authority and government. He disputes His rules and laws, and he encourages rebellion against God.
2. He assures us that disobedience and the violation of God's rules and laws will not result in death, but will be the means to achieve a free and higher way of living and progression towards godhood.
3. He pretends that God withholds from His creatures essential knowledge to keep them ignorant of fundamental issues and a higher and better way of life.
4. With lying words, he encourages distrust, disbelief, and disobedience to God, and he promises to all who will follow him real freedom, with many wonderful blessings and a brilliant future.
5. He presents himself as an angel of light, and as a great benefactor, demanding for himself honor and worship, and showing enmity against Christ and God.

God respects our free choice despite the hazard of misuse. He does not manipulate nor compel us in any way. Satan in contrast, works craftily with deception, falsehood, manipulation, pressure, and violence. In this time of the end one of the most successful deceptions of Satan is found in popular music. In this particular field we will meet and recognize these and similar characteristics about the way Satan works to deceive.

---

18   John 3:16

Chapter 3

Backmasking

In December 1980, John Lennon, a well-known pop star, was shot to death. A number of weeks before this tragedy happened his album *Double Fantasy* was for sale in popular music shops. The song, "Kiss, Kiss, Kiss", from that album, sung by Lennon's wife Yoko Ono, has the sinister backmasked message: "We shot John Lennon."[1]

How is it possible that this message was added to the song? Clearly it was not from Yoko Ono. She definitely did not know that her husband would be shot a number of weeks later. She did not in any way invent the message. While she was singing she did not pronounce such terrible words about her husband. There is only one clear answer, the message must have had another origin.

The backward-spoken secret message was not from any human being; nor was it a heavenly message. Thus there remains only one acceptable explanation that in principle is clearly confirmed. A demon spirit must have spoken it.

Mark David Chapman, the man who killed John Lennon, declared that demonic spirits brought him to this act.[2] No human, but undoubtedly a demonic spirit, spoke weeks in advance: "We shot John Lennon." Chapman, rock fan and Beatles devotee, was used as a medium to perform this sinister act. Knowing the way Satan works, this will not be startling.

Satan delights in controlling the human mind. There are cases

---

1   Jeff Godwin, *What's Wrong with Christian Rock?* p. 144.
2   Jeff Godwin, *The Devil's Disciples,* pp. 86, 87.

where addicted rock fans hear voices in their heads urging them to do awful things, such as using drugs, performing illicit sexual acts, or even committing suicide and murder. A well-known Dutch rock musician, Herman Brood, who admitted that he heard voices, committed suicide on July 11, 2001, when he performed a deadly jump from the roof of Amsterdam's Hilton Hotel.

Did you know that hidden within rock music are a great number of unholy messages that are spoken backwards? They are very common within rock music. When you play the records, CDs, or tapes backwards, you can hear the secret messages. The well-known universal name for this phenomenon is *Backmasking.* Another name is *Communication Reversal.*

Demonic spirits seem to practice this type of backward communication. It appears that this is a satanic principle. Isn't it so significant in this context to note that Britain's leading Satanist, Aleister Crowley (1875–1947), in his book *Manual on Magic,* urged his followers to train themselves to think backwards? He claimed that by practicing writing and speaking backward one can obtain insight into the coming world. This could also be obtained by listening to music and walking backwards.[3]

Crowley was bisexual and had several scandalous affairs. He wanted to become a saint of Satan, and renamed himself as the Great Beast 666. He owned mansions in Italy and Scotland that he used for occultist practices. In his Italian mansion in Cefalù, named *The Abbey of Thelema,* he founded a religious commune. He was expelled from this mansion in 1923 because Italian authorities accused him and his disciples of extreme activities, sexual perversions, luring others into drug abuse, and sacrificing infants in occult rituals. The guitarist Jimmy Page, who owned a large occultist bookstore in London and formed the English Rock band *Led Zeppelin* in 1968, bought the occultist mansion in Scotland and wrote several songs in it, including "Stairway to

---

3   Dan Peters, Steve Peters, and Cher Merrill, *Rock's Hidden Persuader,* p. 57.

Heaven", a popular song with several satanic messages. The song tells of a woman's climb up the stairway to heaven. Some backward messages featured in the song seem to explain that Satan is the one that made the path to go by to heaven and that there is no other way: "There's no escaping it ... Here's to my sweet Satan. No other made a path, for it makes me sad, whose power is Satan."[4] Jimmy explained that he really didn't write the song, but that "Somebody else pushed the pen."[5]

---

4   Ibid., p. 52.
5   Fletcher A. Brothers, *The Rock Report*, p. 54.

Chapter 4

Talking Spirits

The Bible makes it clear that demonic spirits can talk audibly. While on earth Jesus often cured people by casting out evil spirits. At the healing of the demon-possessed in the country of the Gadarenes, the devils spoke and sought to enter into a herd of swine.[1]

This is not a phenomenon limited to the days of Jesus only. Even today there are people possessed by evil spirits. For instance, in the South Pacific one sometimes has to deal with such persons. On the Solomon Islands, as well as on the Fiji Islands, many people still worship spirits.

One of the tasks of the church is to cast out unclean spirits. Christ gave his disciples power to do so. The Gospel according to Matthew says, "And when he had called unto him his twelve disciples, he gave them power against unclean spirits, to cast them out."[2]

Stephen Koncz, a Seventh-day Adventist living in Australia, wrote *Training Manual in Deliverance for Pastors, Elders & Consecrated Church Members*. In it he describes several events of deliverance from demonic possession. There are obstinate and persistent spirits who are not easy to cast out. Earnest prayer and dedication are necessary in order to win the battle.

Although it is not wise to talk with spirits, in one case Koncz exchanged words with a demon. The demon was apologetic and said that he did not want to hurt the one he was in. Koncz said: "'You don't seem like the others I've come across. Jesus warned you about Lucifer, and

---

1   Luke 8:26–39, cf. Matt. 8:28–34; Mark 5:1–20
2   Matt. 10:1

the end result of following him in his rebellion. Why did you follow him? It seems so foolish to me.' Do you know how this demon reacted? Koncz continued, 'This demon hung his head in shame, saying, "You're right; we were deceived. I wish I had not believed Lucifer."'[3] Koncz explained that this was the only time he ever felt sorry for a demon, "Most of them are so nasty and rebellious that it makes you feel disgust towards them."[4] You may think what you like about this event, but isn't it remarkable that this particular demon spirit openly admitted that he had been deceived?

The Bible makes it clear that one third of all the angels fell with Lucifer—with Satan. These deceived angels had nevertheless freely chosen to be on Satan's side in this great controversy.

"I wish I had not believed Lucifer," said the demon. It is too late now for the fallen angels. God's grace is no longer lingering for them. There is no possibility of return. Satan and his angels did not prevail in the heavenly war and they were cast out into the Earth.[5]

The great controversy between good and evil is continuing upon this Earth. Millions of people are deceived and misled. However, it is not yet too late for human beings who are still alive. "I wish I had not believed Lucifer." We may be thankful that salvation is still possible for us. Let us seriously make use of that golden opportunity before it is too late for us as well.

---

3   I asked Stephen whether he could see and observe this demon, or whether he inferred this from what the demon was saying. His answer was: "No, I didn't see the demon who hung his head in shame, and it is as you wrote, just my inference from his voice. He seemed truly sad about the deception. I don't think that there are many demons like this one, by the way. Most whom I've encountered in people as we pray for their deliverance are angry and very anti-Christ, extremely stubborn and totally unrepentant. Even this one who admitted he was deceived was not repentant, as all the demons have gone way past that point in grieving away the Holy Spirit. Repentance is impossible in the later stages of deliberate transgression."

4   Stephen Koncz, *Training Manual in Deliverance*, p. 43.

5   Rev. 12:4, 7–9

Chapter 5

A Great Musician

Satan is, according to the Bible, a great and skillful musician. The prophet Ezekiel, describing his musical abilities, says: "the workmanship of thy tabrets and of thy pipes was prepared in thee in the day that thou wast created."[1] Satan undoubtedly possessed a great natural talent for music. This gift was prepared in him on the day that he was created.

Ellen G. White (1827–1915) was a remarkable woman who lived a dedicated Christian life closely connected with God. As a sincere student of the Bible, she received a great deal of spiritual insight and there is clear evidence that God blessed her with the prophetic gift of prophecy.[2] She wrote many books and articles that are still highly valued and appreciated today.

When writing about Satan's original position as musical leader in heaven, Ellen White states:

> The hour for joyful, happy songs of praise to God and His dear Son had come. Satan had led the heavenly choir. He had raised the first note; then all the angelic host had united with him, and glorious strains of music had resounded through heaven in honor of God and His dear Son.[3]

1   Ezek. 28:13
2   Before the day of the Lord comes, God promises to pour out His Spirit. The gift of prophecy will be revealed and God will give dreams and visions (Joel 2:28–31).
3   Ellen G. White, *The Story of Redemption*, p. 25.

The enemy knows how desirable a place heaven is to every human being. He has a keen sense of what he has lost; and when he was cast out of heaven ... he knows that the Scriptures will be fulfilled, and that a host that no man can number will encircle the throne where he so often stood as chorister, to sing songs of praise and adoration to God and the Lamb.[4]

The cause of Satan's fall was his coveting of the honor and glory of Christ. He demanded equal status and authority with the Son of God. Ellen White explains:

Little by little Lucifer came to indulge the desire for self-exaltation ... Instead of seeking to make God supreme in the affections and allegiance of all created beings, it was his endeavor to secure their service and loyalty to himself ... The preference shown to Christ he declared an act of injustice both to himself and to all the heavenly host, and announced that he would no longer submit to this invasion of his rights and theirs. He would never again acknowledge the supremacy of Christ. He had determined to claim the honor which should have been given him, and take command of all who would become his followers; and he promised those who would enter his ranks a new and better government, under which all would enjoy freedom.[5]

Satan's fall is significant. With him his music fell also. The prophet Isaiah said, "Thy pomp is brought down to the grave, and the noise of thy viols."[6] We can be sure that Satan's worldly musical noises will continue to the very end. As he endeavors to secure the service and loyalty of all created beings for himself, we need not be surprised to

---

4   Ellen G. White, *The Youth's Instructor*, October 26, 1899.
5   Ellen G. White, *Patriarchs and Prophets*, pp. 35, 40.
6   Isa. 14:11.

find in many popular songs secret messages that glorify him and defy Christ.

LaMar Boschman, musician, author, and preacher from Bedford, Texas, explains Satan's fallen music in these words:

> Music that once was used to worship Almighty God now became music of an earthly nature, it became the music of the world and began to appeal to our lower nature instead of appealing to God and our spiritual man … That anointed and powerful ministry of music that Lucifer had in heaven is now corrupted … He still has the same powerful ministry to create worship … and Lucifer uses that ministry to get worship for himself because he craves it.[7]

Thus, we need not be surprised when we find in unholy music secret messages that honor and glorify Satan, and defy a dedicated spiritual life with faith in God. Satan is very pleased when he can enter churches unexpectedly and unnoted through modern popular Christian music and songs in order to exert his counterfeit Christian influence.

---

7   LaMar Boschman, *The Rebirth of Music*, p. 16.

Chapter 6

Rock Music

Satan pulls out all the stops in his severe and desperate struggle against God. A particularly successful tool for misleading many people is rock music. Several rock stars openly admit that their music is satanic and that they are led and inspired by supernatural powers or spirits.[1]

John McLaughlin, British rock guitarist and leader of the electric jazz-rock *Mahavishnu Orchestra* (1970), testifies, "One night we were playing and suddenly the spirit entered into me, and I was playing, but it was no longer me playing."[2]

Rock band *Led Zeppelin* produced the song "Stairway to Heaven," a very popular hit with several backmasking messages such as: "Play backwards. Hear words sung. Here's to my sweet Satan. He will give those with him 666. There was a little tool shed where he made us suffer, sad Satan. There was a little child born naked... now I am Satan. I will sing because I live with Satan." This song is said to be one of the greatest rock songs in the history of rock and roll.

Former group vocalist Robert Plant said, "'Stairway' gets the best reactions of anything we do." [3] Jimmy Page, the most prominent member of the group, explained that, "...the song was written in only 15 minutes... He added that it felt as if a presence were actually 'guiding their pencil across the page.'"[4]

---

1   John Blanchard and Dan Lucarini, *Can We Rock the Gospel?* pp. 80, 81.
2   Brothers, *The Rock Report*, p. 58.
3   Peters, Peters, and Merrill, *What About Christian Rock?* p. 51.
4   Ibid.

David Bowie, a well-known and influential rock musician, declares that, "Rock has always been the devil's music. You can't convince me that it isn't. I honestly believe everything that I've said—I believe Rock and Roll is dangerous."[5]

Rock pioneer Little Richard, American musician, singer, songwriter, recording actor and artist, was for many years the musical model for several rock stars. His full name is Richard Wayne Penniman. He was born in 1932. As is usual with most rock stars, Richard used drugs and lived an outrageously immoral life. He was also a bisexual man.

However, the voice of his conscience became strong and in 1957 he decided to live a Christian life and enrolled in Oakwood College, a Seventh-day Adventist institution in Huntsville, Alabama. Soon he started to travel around as an evangelist, but unfortunately the pressure of rock fans and his contact in 1960 with *the Beatles* during a trip to England influenced him to return to his rock career.

Again, around 1978 and 1979, he turned his back on rock and resumed his evangelistic activities. During this period he confessed:

> My true belief about Rock'N'Roll—and there have been a lot of phrases attributed to me over the years—is this: I believe this kind of music is demonic ... A lot of the beats in music today are taken from voodoo, from the voodoo drums. If you study music in rhythms, like I have, you'll see that is true. I believe that kind of music is driving people from Christ. It is contagious...[6]

Ozzy Osbourne, a devil worshiper who was until 1980 the lead singer for the group *Black Sabbath*, confessed, "I know that there is

5   Rolling Stone, February 12, 1976, p. 83; cf. John Makujina, *Measuring the Music,* p. 249, and Brothers, *The Rock Report,* p. 26.

6   Charles White, *The Life and Times of Little Richard,* p. 197; cf. Fischer, *The Battle for Christian Music,* pp. 74, 75 and Godwin, *Dancing with Demons,* p. 41.

some supernatural force using me to bring forth my rock and roll."[7]
He also said, "I don't know if I'm a medium for some outside source.
Whatever it is, frankly, I hope it's not what I think...Satan."[8]

Tim Fischer, a musician and teacher with an unusual blend of musical knowledge, skill, and experience, explains:

> The satanic connection for a large number of rock musicians is undeniable. Why put our heads in the sand?
> We do not charge that Christian rock musicians are consciously serving Satan; but by modelling their music after
> these unholy rock bands, they are opening up to Satan an
> avenue he has never enjoyed before in our churches.[9]

An interesting, but for some a controversial source on Satanism,
are the books written by Rebecca Brown, who was a Christian medical
doctor at Ball Memorial Hospital, New Castle, Indiana. Rebecca wrote
one of her books together with Elaine, who had at one time served
Satan, but had since decided to accept Christ. Because of the stunning
information, a number of people doubt the validity of Rebecca's book.[10]

Some doubt Rebecca's claim that there are secret satanic communities in America performing evil works, rituals, and sacrifices at
meetings out in the country in solitary places where Satan sometimes
appears. Others have doubts because they find it difficult to believe
Rebecca's teaching that even Christians can be inhabited by demons.
However, others defend her books as being truthful and some testify

---

7 Hubert T. Spence, *Confronting Contemporary Christian Music*, p. 98.
8 Brothers, *The Rock Report,* pp. 63, 64.
9 Fischer, *The Battle for Christian Music*, p. 75.
10 For instance, when reading Roger J. Morneau's book, *A Trip into the Supernatural*, which was published by the Review and Herald Publishing Association in 1982 and 1993, a number of people may also doubt some of the wonderful facts he describes as well.

that they were greatly helped and blessed by them.[11]

One of those blessed by Rebecca's book, *He came to Set the Captives Free,* is Sanaa, a woman from Atlanta, Georgia. She writes:

> This book must be read under the leading and prayfulness of God's Holy Spirit. If you encounter any attempt to stop you from reading this book … get yourself a prayer warrior, to pray over you and for you, receive the blessing that satan will keep his hands off you and that the Spirit of God will illuminate your mind. Then pick up this book with your Bible and read in anticipation of receiving another one of God's great blessing upon your life. The cloud will be lifted after your reading, accepting, and practical application of this book's writings … If you are desiring to learn basic principals of spiritual warfare, or you are coming out of hard-core Satanism, New Age, or Witchcraft, this is a survival manual for you! Just remember with God all things are possible, and persevere in the power of His might! He is faithful! And you will overcome!

Whatever people may think, there are interesting facts described in Rebecca's books that are also supported by other sources. The story goes that Rebecca met Elaine at Memorial Hospital, where she was stricken ill by demonic powers. With a mission to influence and destroy a certain church, Elaine had come into contact with Christians who prayed for her. The demons were unable to interfere. From that moment on Elaine considered becoming a Christian and an intensive struggle with the demonic powers followed.

Elaine was born to poor parents in a home without peace. Her

---

11   Rebecca's books were first published in 1986 and 1987 by Chick Publications. Jack Chick and Rebecca Brown decided to end their business relationship, but Jack still defends Rebecca and the truthfulness of her books. Rebecca's books were reprinted in the early nineties by Whitaker House, New Kensington, PA. Rebecca and her husband hold *Harvest Warriors* speaking engagements all over the country.

father was a drunkard and her mother was not a Christian. Elaine's birth was assisted by a nurse who belonged to *The Brotherhood*, a Satan-worshiping cult, and she paved the way that led Elaine, while she was still a young girl, into the Satanist cult by the invitation of Sandy, Elaine's best friend. Sandy invited Elaine to a youth camp run by *The Brotherhood* and there Elaine was trained to receive the power of Satan and to serve him. Thus, early in life Elaine's body was opened up as a home for demons. At a special secret meeting she cut her finger, dipped a pen in the drops of her own blood, and signed a contract, promising to give her body, soul, and spirit to her father Satan, the "master of the universe," in return for many "wonderful blessings."

Elaine became a high priestess and bride of Satan and served her master with total commitment for a period of seventeen years. As a representative of Satan, and as communicated to her by him, she made many trips on a mission to advance his cause. Through her many contacts with demonic powers and personal involvement she gained a great deal of insight in the working schemes and trick methods that Satan uses to reach his goals.

It is interesting that with regard to music, Elaine testifies frankly, "Rock music is Satan's music … the whole movement of rock music was carefully planned and carried out by Satan and his servants from its very beginning. Rock music didn't 'just happen,' it was a carefully masterminded plan by none other than Satan himself."[12]

Elaine notes that she has personally met many of the well-known rock music stars. She says, "They all signed contracts with Satan in return for fame and fortune... These rock stars know exactly what they are doing. They are, step by step, teaching untold millions of young people to worship and serve Satan."[13] Is it any wonder that rock music contains all kinds of secret demonic messages?

Note the following:

---

12   Rebecca Brown, *Prepare for War,* p. 141.
13   Rebecca Brown, *He Came to Set the Captives Free,* p. 63, 146.

Elaine attended special ceremonies at various recording studios throughout the U.S. for the specific purpose of placing satanic blessings on the rock music recorded. She and others did incantations which placed demons on EVERY record and tape of rock music sold. At times they also called up special demons who spoke on the recordings—especially in the various backmasked messages. Also, in many, many of the recordings, the Satanists themselves were recorded in the background (masked by the over-all noise of the music) doing chants and incantations to summon up more demons every time one of the records or tapes or videos is played.[14]

At this point we may pause for a moment and ask ourselves, what is the result of all this and how are we to judge such a scenario? Is there any evidence that sustains this report? In light of Rebecca's assertions it may not startle us when we consider the dramatic results of Rock music. We are often confronted with outrageous outbursts of violence and vandalism that accompany some Rock concerts. With the blessing that Satan has bestowed on Rock music, is it any wonder that youngsters who listen to such music are often lawless and rebellious, showing immoral and anti-Christian behavior?

When Christian Rock is played in church and other decent places, these characteristics may not as readily show up. The unruly results of Christian Rock may not so quickly and clearly be discerned since Satan can also appear as an angel of light and choose, in a Christian context, a more refined strategy that includes a false feeling of spirituality.

Andrew, his second name is not mentioned, is a former Rock singer who, before turning his back on his Rock career, was totally given up to this kind of demonic music. However, when he started to pray and read the Bible it completely changed his life. He lists some of the disastrous fruits of Rock music and knows by experience that evil spirits

14   Ibid, p. 146.

are at work. He affirms that through the mysterious involvement of evil
spirits, satanic backward messages turned up in some of their songs.
This happened without their participation. He also affirms that some
bands or singers after the recording of the songs officiate some kind
of "blessing" during which Satan is invoked. Here is part of Andrew's
testimony:

> The rock music has been the center of my life for seven
> years. I did what I could possibly do in order to become
> somebody and I can say that I succeeded. But the mo-
> ment I felt that God really exist I understood that I had
> to follow His way and not the one I had chosen. But I was
> so attached to my band, that it was impossible for me to
> leave it. When I started to warmly and sincerely pray, I saw
> that step by step my life was changing every passing day.
> I opened the door of my soul to Christ, Who was knock-
> ing on it and I understood that through my life until that
> moment I glorified Satan and not God. Indeed, only near
> God can anyone feel the true happiness and accomplishes
> his life. In my case the change didn't occur at once. When I
> found out what is hidden behind the rock music, I realized
> that my whole life was in contradiction with God's will,
> I felt qualms of conscience. I was quite lost, I made the
> decision to totally follow God. Here is a great mystery: the
> decision to change our life belongs to us, but the power
> to do it comes from God. We can receive this help from
> God through prayer. That is why we have to pray from
> the bottom of our hearts: "My Lord, help me escape from
> the devil' trap, because I now understand that this is not a
> play, as I thought at the beginning....
>
> The Holy Scripture also warns us: "You will recog-
> nize them by their fruits" (Matthew 7,16). Which are the
> fruits of the rock stars? Revolt, drugs, death, alcoholism,

violence, homosexuality and sexual libertinism. In the early 80's there appeared within the rock music a phenomenon which couldn't be completely explained until today. This phenomenon is called reversed rendering. At the reversed rendering of some rock songs, there are heard messages which usually have a strong Satanist feature. Blasphemies against Christ, words of praise for Satan or immoral advice. This phenomenon was signaled by many researchers and cannot be denied. Technically speaking, these messages are almost impossible to be deliberately accomplished. How can anyone sing a verse or a sentence, and the reversed rendering to have another meaning, with Satanic content? This is what happened with some of our songs, without our participation in this sense. The only explanation we can give in this case is that this phenomenon takes place with the mysterious involvement of the evil spirits. We have proves that some bands or singers, after the recording in the studio and before the multiplication of the, matrita usually officiate some kind of "blessing", during which they invoke Satan to help them enjoy success. The way priests bless and the bred during the Church divine service, the same the servants of black magic have their ceremonies of invoking the devil.…

I do beg you to be careful what kind of music you listen to and do not misunderstand me, I do not condemn music in general; there also is good music, but you have to look for it in nowadays society.[15]

Rebecca continues her report:

As the music is played, these demons are called into the

---

15   Orthodox Advices, "The mysteries of music." http://www.sfaturiortodoxe.ro/ orthodox/orthodox_advices_rock_music.htm (accessed on May 1, 2013).

room to afflict the person playing the music and anyone else who is listening … Many of the song lyrics are themselves actual incantations calling up demons when the song is sung… The purpose of all of this? *Mind control!* Mind control not only to give the listeners understanding of the messages about Satan conveyed to them by the music, but also to prevent them from recognizing their need for Jesus and the salvation He died on the cross to give us.[16]

You may wonder of what importance this is to those who already know that rock music and pop concerts are not good for our spiritual well-being. The problem is that even for those people, there are certain sly and ostensibly good and harmless influential developments that took place long ago and are still in operation.

---

16   Rebecca Brown, *He Came to Set the Captives Free*, p. 146, emphasis original.

Chapter 7

Drastic Changes

A new kind of culture has come into being. We now live in the twenty-first century, the Age of Aquarius, which is to be an era in which everything should go differently; socially, economically and spiritually. Humanity is supposed to be regarded as one big brotherhood. One world religion should be aimed at in which all different people with their pluralistic features and cultures should feel at home. Many church leaders declare that drastic changes must take place in order to function adequately in this modern age.

The modern church should undergo what is called, a *paradigm shift*. Church services should no longer be so focused on divine standards, Biblical truths, and dogmas, but rather on generally accepted cultural standards and principles. This shift is a necessary step in order to reach people and enhance church growth. An important feature in the process of this shift is the idea that the old beloved church hymns are out of favor, and that modern songs, popular music, Contemporary Christian music, and praise bands should be used instead. Another *paradigm shift* idea is that a new kind of mystical spirituality, known as *contemplative spirituality,* should be advocated and practiced, as well as modern *meditational disciplines.*

This new way of thinking and practicing church is a reflection of postmodernism, a movement that is often associated with difference, plurality, textuality, and skepticism. There is also a close link with the New Age movement.

A main characteristic of postmodernism is that long cherished truths, ideas, and methods are to be mistrusted. Things are viewed in a relative way. Truth is seen only from a cultural context and our perception of truth and the essence of truth are relative. The result of postmodern thinking is that cherished certainties are undermined, while many people are anxiously seeking substitutes that will pacify their minds. The effects of this modern way of thinking are clearly seen in many churches, where a tendency towards change and innovation has captured many church leaders.

Generally, the idea has taken root that the church can't be successful by following the old paths any longer. New forms of worship must be introduced into the churches. Forms that are adapted to the times that we live in. The trusted church services that we are accustomed to are now regarded as dull, boring, and outmoded.

Thus, a new modern type of church came into being, the *Emerging Church,* which favors new ways of undertaking church services and stresses the use of a simple story and narrative, instead of preaching. It's a popular, ecumenically oriented conversational church, committed to dialogue, but not firmly based on Scriptural truth.

The idea is that if the church is to remain significant and be able to influence our modern society, it must keep up with the times. Therefore, the argument is made that music in church should be adapted and modernized; otherwise it will be impossible to keep the young people from leaving. The music that they are used to hearing in the secular world should also be presented in church. Under this reasoning, Christian rock music was introduced into the church's worship services.

The introduction of Christian rock is certainly worrying for many faithful believers in the church. For instance, a deacon who was a fan of rock music before he accepted Christ, testifies, "The first thing that God did in my heart was to set me free from this kind of music. However, it is so sad to see how the devil manages to persuade the believers to use this same music in God's House!"[1]

---

1   John Blanchard and Dan Lucarini, *Can We Rock the Gospel?* p. 23.

Jack Wheaton, who holds a doctorate degree in music, says, "Sadly, we have let the wily fox, Satan, into our sanctuaries in our desperate efforts to attract teenagers and worldly adults to our worship services."[2]

---

2   Wheaton, *Crisis in Christian Music,* pp. 35, 36.

Chapter 8

No Difference

Modern church-growth movements consciously emphasize the need for Christian rock. However, let it be clear that this music is in fact similar to what is heard in the world. Only the words differ. It is worldly music with Christian lyrics.

John Blanchard, author and teacher, wrote a book on rock music together with Dan Lucarini, a musician and businessman. They clearly point out, "As evidenced here, there is essentially no difference between the rock music written and performed by secular artists or by Christian artists. Stylistically and musically, they are exactly the same."[1] It is often thought that religious words make rock music acceptable for Christians. Gradually, with this mistaken perception, Christian rock music has emerged.

However, if the church applies popular music techniques that produce worldly passion, as well as forms of hypnotic ecstasy and mass hysteria, will this then be dispelled when Christian words are sung? If drumbeat rhythms incite demonic powers, can we by using other lyrics with these or similar rhythms invite the power of God with heavenly peacefulness? In Jack Wheaton's music ministry he warns, "It is a dangerous mistake to think that you can take the rock format, add Christian lyrics, and everything will be okay."[2]

The boisterous and unruly appearance of some modern Christian revival meetings speak to us in loud, clear language. Juanita McElwain,

---

1   Blanchard and Lucarini, *Can We Rock the Gospel?* p. 71.
2   Wheaton, *Crisis in Christian Music*, p. 64.

professor of music therapy at Eastern New Mexico University and Phillips University Enid, Oklahoma, writes:

> 'Christian rock' is a misnomer. Who has ever heard of Christian whiskey, Christian pornography, Christian adultery, or Christian x-rated movies? There is no Christian rock. As I have demonstrated scores of times before large audiences, the measurable physiological effects of rock music, whether labelled Christian or otherwise, are identical and clinically undesirable. That is because the music is the same, no matter the label. It is all a part of the same counterfeit and has the same effects on participants and listeners.[3]

> Once more she affirms in clear language, "The music and all of its effects are the same, whatever the label. Christian rock and other rock groups look alike and sound alike. The psycho physiological effects of Christian rock and other rock do not differ from each other, and both share the same undesirable stress-causing factors in relation to the digestive, respiratory, circulatory, and neurological systems of the body. They both have similar psychological effects and also share addictive features." [4]

There is clearly no difference between the effects of Christian rock and worldly rock music. It is perfectly understandable why many good believers are embarrassed about modern Christian rock music in the church. However, almost as a rule, their concern is met with the shallow terms that music is neutral—it is a matter of taste or choice—it is what you are used to and what you prefer—it is just a

---

3   Juanita McElwain, *The Lord is My Song*, p. 107.
4   Ibid., p. 108.

matter of what you like.[5]

We are repeatedly told that we have to keep up with the times that we are living in.. If the church prefers a secure future, not wanting to be out of step, modern adjustments have to be made. How else do you think the church can grow? How would you keep the younger generation in the church? These are the kind of arguments that are repeated time after time.

---

5   Music is never neutral. It excites feelings and reactions either for good or bad. Taste or preference does not count here. A combination of good words with unholy music does not make the music holy, it defiles the good.

Chapter 9

Luther and Wesley

Sometimes Martin Luther and John Wesley are used as examples of godly people who used contemporary music for their hymns. It is argued that Luther also used contemporary music. This is incorrect! Luther made use of only one contemporary melody in the year 1535 and when he realized that this melody could somehow have an unholy tinge he promptly composed another melody for his hymn.[1]

If, however, sincere Reformers sometimes used popular melodies, the fact remains that we are not justified to follow human beings and make them the criterion on which we base our religious practices. Furthermore, at the time of the Reformation there was not as big a difference between popular and sacred music. Therefore, it can hardly be compared to the modern rock music that we know in our time.

John Makujina, teacher and author of several articles in academic journals, rightly explains, "Nevertheless, the difference between the secular and sacred at the time was not easily distinguishable in that music in the medieval period had predominantly ecclesiastical origins and orientation."[2]

Edwin Liemohn, researcher and author of several books on music, also wrote, "Those who taught and those who studied [music] were associated with the work of the church and many melodies written for

---

1   Dan Lucarini, *Why I Left the Contemporary Christian Music Movement*, p. 107; David W. Cloud, *Contemporary Christian Music under the Spotlight*, pp. 160, 161.

2   Makujina, *Measuring the Music*, p. 229.

secular texts were produced by the same men who wrote melodies for church use." [3]

John Wesley was also very careful with what music and melodies he used in his meetings. In his conclusion Makujina states that the example of the Wesleyans, "does far more to undermine CCM's position than it does to buttress it."[4] It is clear that the Wesleyans cannot rightly be used as a positive and favorable example to appropriate secular styles of music, such as Contemporary Christian music, in church or for evangelistic purposes.

Steven Darsey, who holds a doctoral degree of musical arts in choral conducting from the Yale Institute of Sacred Music, says, "No reasonable interpretation of the facts can justify in the name of John Wesley the freewheeling use of nearly any song that strikes the fancy of modern worship."[5]

The modern mega churches all use Christian rock music and they appear to be very successful. It works! As is contended, they have at least discovered a method to win the postmodern generation to the church. As a result, the methods used by the mega churches are promoted and introduced. With this modern approach, church leaders think they can benefit the church and accomplish a great work for God in this world. What a big lie this is!

On the surface it may seem to be very successful, but the results must always be faithfully measured by Biblical standards, without being led astray by personal feelings, choice, or preference. The question of whether God is really glorified by these modern approaches and revivals is crucial and must always be considered seriously.

---

3   Ibid.; cf. Edwin Liemohn, *The Chorale*, pp. 12, 13.
4   Makujina, *Measuring the Music*, p. 241.
5   Steven Darsey, *The Hymn: A Journal of Congregational Song*, p. 20.

Chapter 10

Secret Messages

In the world, rock music often contains various kinds of secret messages—messages that originate with demonic spirits. This is a well-known fact that is openly attested to by several rock musicians and other knowledgeable people in this area.[1]

Some backward messages are clearly audible, while others are more or less difficult to make out. Not all backward messages are plainly demonic phrases. Neither are all of these necessarily the result of demonic activity.

In a very few rare cases a backward message could have been purposely inserted technically, although this would take a tremendous amount of effort to perform. In one or two other cases it may be just the result of singing unknowingly one or two words of which the sound, when listened backwards, happen to make some sense and could possibly be interpreted as a message. However, it may be clear that this is extremely exceptional and when this is at all performed purposely, it requires a tremendous lot of ingenuity, skill and time, that in no way answers to the backward messages that are hidden in Rock music.

Some people don't believe that backward messages exist. They think it is all nonsense and just a matter of imagination. But the rock music producers are well aware of this real phenomenon and some have a note published about it on the album cover.

---

1   Elaine explains that "at times we also called up special demons who spoke on the recordings the various backmasked messages" ("A Satanist Testifies About Rock," New Covenant Ministries, http://www.nccg.org/occult/Occult022-Rock2.html [accessed May 6, 2013].

On the cover of Motley Crew's album *Shout at the Devil,* is the warning, "This record may contain backward masking." At one point on the album are the words, "Backward mask where you are, oh, lost in error, Satan." The purpose and meaning of this cryptic satanic message may be to implant in the subconscious mind a feeling of despondency. Instead of man rejoicing about the redemptive message of the Gospel, Satan delights in making people feel lost and miserable, a phenomenon that also pervades his own mind.

The rock group, *Styx,* from Chicago, also has on its album, *Paradise Theatre,* the written message that there is backmasking. The song, "Snowblind", has the intriguing and inviting backward message, "Oh Satan, move in our voices."[2]

Although I am not fond of rock music, or of hearing backward messages, I can admit that I have heard a couple of clear messages myself in Led Zeppelin's song *Stairway to Heaven.* I know I am not the only one who believes that demonic influences are revealed in rock music and in similar popular music genres. Even Rock stars like David Bowie and Little Richard openly admitted that Rock music is demonic.

With a closer look at the modern rock groups these satanic phenomena can easily be discerned. Alan Gourley, a prolific Australian author and researcher, wrote that:

> It is very doubtful if any singer or group could get to the top of the pop scene today without first accepting satanism. If by chance a newcomer makes a hit record, then it will likely be a 'one and only' unless the satanic cult followers are satisfied ... Rock music is primitive; by its own nature it arouses primitive, self-destructive passions and its disciples promote every depravity. It is the music of depravity; the jungle beat of voodoo, demons and human sacrifice ... Satanism is known to practice the backwards expression of messages and so it can not be considered

2   Brothers, *The Rock Report,* pp. 62, 86.

coincidental that the use of subliminals and backmasking find themselves at home with the Rock music and disco scene ... The spirit of evil is much more prevalent in this world today than the spirit of good; it is easier to lead people wrong than to lead them right.[3]

Some may continue to argue that the music producers are the ones who inserted all of the backward messages. As alluded to earlier, this could only be true in a very few rare cases. Modern multitrack recording could make it theoretically possible to record a sound and then insert it backward, but this is not easily done. Bruce Helmic, chief recording engineer for Amerisound Studios in Columbus, Ohio, comments, "Backward masking does exist, but it's very rare. At studio rates," the sound techs contends, 'it's very expensive because of the technical trouble involved in doing it well enough so that you can't hear it when played forward.'"[4]

So the reader can see that this troublesome technical effort to insert a backward message is not likely to happen on a regular basis. Therefore this theory cannot possibly account for the scores of backward messages that turn up in various albums.

Dan and Steve Peters, founders of Solid Rock Ministries, and Cher Merrill, author, have done a lot of research on rock music. In 1979 they held their first rock music seminar. Since then they have presented it numerous times in more than 35 states. They claim that hidden messages on many albums have been confirmed.[5] They explain:

The complexity of some of these hidden messages seems to defy human innovation. It seems feasible, therefore, that the supernatural has sometimes been at work without the knowledge of the rock musicians or the recording technicians ... Who, then, do we suspect is doing so much

---

3   Alan Gourley, "Singing Death," in *Assault on Childhood*, chap. 3.

4   Peters, Peters, and Merrill, *Rock's Hidden Persuader*, p. 56.

5   Peters, Peters, and Merrill, *Rock's Hidden Persuader*, p. 37.

of this covert communications?... There is no reason to believe therefore, that Satan can't serve up a secret message on a record if and when he wishes, since through this technique, he could receive worship from many unknowing fans ... Whether these messages are Satan-created, or simply Satan-inspired, subliminal stimuli certainly must have the 'Satanic Seal of Approval,' for one never hears of secular rock albums promoting secretly the gospel of Christ—or even simply wholesome thoughts ... And while the notion of satanic involvement may sound archaic in our modern, technological society, any military strategist will tell you it is dangerous to underestimate the enemy—and foolhardy to pretend he doesn't exist. Satan would love for us to misjudge his powers or activities, or better yet, scorn his existence. After all, he is the master of disguise, and backmasking seems to be a perfect avenue for his trickery. Therefore, although a certain amount of wisdom is needed to forestall a 'witch hunt' mentality, it's still perfectly logical to assume satanic involvement in backmasking.[6]

But what about the Contemporary Christian music presented in the churches? Are the halls of the sanctuary safe from the influences of demonic spirits? The truth is very alarming. Research has shown that many demonic secret messages are also present in Christian rock music.

Jeff Godwin, an American specialist in the field of rock music, was a slave to this kind of music for thirteen years. After becoming a Christian he dedicated his life to a ministry of researching and exposing the dangers in rock music. He currently travels around the world presenting a series of five live rock music seminars to churches and other groups.

---

6   Ibid., pp. 56, 57, 59, 60.

He states that, "Hundreds of satanic backmasks are buried in 'Christian' Rock and CCM music. Yes, you read it right. Popular CCM music contains literally HUNDREDS of subliminal messages and commands glorifying Satan/Lucifer."[7]

This may sound exaggerated, but there are certainly a number of hidden messages present. Keith Piper, an Australian pastor, founder of the Liberty Bible Institute in Sydney, Australia, and a former church planter in Africa, presents a similar picture. Several examples of demonic messages that are sung are given, such as Ozzy Osborne's song "Nativity in Black": "Now I have you with me under my power … You'll see who I am, my name is Lucifer, please take my hand." Also, Iron Maiden's song "Number of the Beast": "I'll possess your body and I'll make you burn."[8]

As for Christian Rock, Piper reports, "C-rock contains demon messages backmasked praising Satan."[9]

It has been claimed that "Christian Rock Albums [are] loaded with demonics."[10] Here are some examples to make this clear:

- STRYPER's album, *In God We Trust,* contains the hidden messages, "Hail Lucifer—Satan who love we worship."

- DANIEL BAND's album, *Rise Up,* has the hidden words, "Now worship Satan—I shall love Satan—I am fighting back oh master demon."

- JERUSALEM's album, *In His Majesty's Service,* is backmasked with the words, "Hey Lord Satan—Yarrh Satan he's master—Yarrh, Satan is Lord—Say

---

7   Godwin, *What's Wrong with Christian Rock,* p. 127, emphasis original.
8   Keith Piper, "Stairway to Hell," *Answers Book,* chap. 79.
9   Ibid., "'Christian' Rock Music: What's Wrong With 'Christian' Rock Music?", chap. 98.
10   "The Prince of the Power of the Air He Is In Your Music," Babylon Forsaken Ministries, http://www.babylonforsaken.com/devilsmusic.html (accessed May 29, 2013).

I love you Satan—Jesus God He serves Satan—Oh we're yours Satan evil, oh evil, God is nil—My friend Lucifer sings for you."

- RESURRECTION BAND's album, *Between Heaven 'n Hell*, is backmasked with, "Yeah Lucifer promised me more—Live for a week—Ooh evil I take the mark."

- PETRA, another Christian rock group, while singing *Washes Whiter Than Snow*, had no idea they were being backmasked with the shocking hidden refrain, "Ooh so evil—Lord Satan—Lord Satan my love." Each of these phrases is repeated over and over again.

- CARMEN's record, *Destination is There*, has the hidden words, "Satan worship the mark—worship Satan." Also on their album, *Radically Saved*, is the backmasked message, "Here's Lucifer."[11]

When confronted with this phenomenon many Christians, church leaders, and pastors don't feel at ease. Some don't want to speak about it. A number become irritated and sometimes even angry. Others try to brush it aside, deny, or ignore the facts and come up with excuses that this is the way to keep the church attractive and relevant nowadays. They explain that we live in an imperfect world and sometimes have to choose a less favorable solution that may not satisfy everybody. However, this is not the way it should go. God requires serious and complete dedication and no halfhearted, compromised service. The church should approach this issue courageously. They need to earnestly pray about it, study the impact of this kind of music carefully with an open mind, provide ample information, and act accordingly. That is the only way that God will bless and approve. He will never sanction a

---

11   Ibid. Also, "The Devil Is REALLY in the Music," Christian Research Service, http://www.christianresearchservice.com/the-prince-of-the-power-of-the-air-he-is-in-your-music/ (accessed May 29, 2013). Cf. McElwain, *The Lord is My Song*, pp. 73, 74.

way that tends to cover up the truth and that will keep people ignorant.

It certainly is a very serious issue. Imagine people coming together in church to worship God. However, the credo is that this should be done in our modern age in a contemporary way; otherwise it would not be possible to keep people in the church, especially teenagers. Therefore, God must be praised with Contemporary Christian music, with nearly everyone thinking that our heavenly Father is honored with this modern style of music.

Many feel that popular music must be tolerated for the sake of the youth. However, the path of tolerance leads to the highway of acceptance, and that is Satan's purpose. He knows that in reality, he will be praised and honored in church with this kind of music. Although many people may not be aware of this or realize the true situation, this demonic phenomenon is nevertheless present and defiling the service that is meant to glorify God. Satan will have secured his end when God withholds His blessing.

Rick Warren, pastor of the Saddleback Church is one of America's most influential preacher, has undoubtedly played a role in undermining the difference between Christian and worldly values in music. He surprised the 30,000 members and visitors present in Angel Stadium at Anaheim, California, on Sunday, April 17, 2005, when he announced, "I've always wanted to do this in this stadium." He then sang an impersonation of the late rock star Jimi Hendrix's hit song "Purple Haze." This late occult rock musician, who had been an avid student of occult literature, use to communicate regularly with demon spirits. Nevertheless, the audience erupted into laughter and the church band joined in playing back-up to Warren's singing.[12]

Warren even dares to contend that, "God loves all kinds of music because he invented it all … God likes variety and enjoys it all."[13] Warren emphasizes and overvalues modern music to the extent that he

---

12   Blanchard and Lucarini, *Can We Rock the Gospel?* pp. 94, 147, 148.
13   Rick Warren, *The Purpose Driven Life*, pp. 65, 66.

claims church-growth is dependent upon it. He states, "It may also be *the* most influential factor in determining who[m] your church reaches for Christ and whether or not your church grows."[14]

However, are people not drawn by the clear preaching of God's Word and the conviction wrought by the Holy Spirit? Is the power of God's Word with the working of the Spirit not *the* most influential factor that brings people to Christ?

The *only* and *most* influential factor for real church-growth and bringing people to Christ does not come from the music, but from God. Jesus plainly declared, "No man can come to me, except the Father which hath sent me draw him."[15]

The dramatic results of overvaluing contemporary music is that in many churches popular Christian rock bands play unholy music and sing popular Christian songs.[16] However, it is to be expected, as Ellen White indicates, that the angels of God withdraw with sadness when unholy music and songs are presented, and demonic spirits have free play.[17]

Could it then be possible that demons sing along unnoticed with their malignant words? Could it be that they cleverly and imperceptibly mingle their secret demonic messages with the popular Christian songs performed?

It has been suggested that the rock rhythm and style is in itself an invocation to demonic powers to participate. "If demons are invoked

---

14   Warren, *The Purpose Driven Church*, p. 280.
15   John 6:44.
16   "Thousands of praise bands have since taken his (Warren's) advice and made rock music the nearly-universal music style in the global church." Blanchard and Lucarini, *Can We Rock the Gospel?* p. 17.
17   Ellen White pointed out that, "every time the church assembles, angels of God are present and evil angels are also present" (Ellen G. White, *The Early Elmshaven Years*, vol. 5, p. 74). She also stated that Satan, "is in attendance when men assemble for the worship of God. Though hidden from sight, he is working with all diligence to control the minds of the worshipers" (*The Great Controversy*, p. 518). She also described a meeting of Christians where the sound of vocal and instrumental music was heard with a frivolous song while the angels of God with sadness were moving away (*Testimonies for the Church*, vol. 1, p. 506).

through Rock then it is understandable that they will sing in duo with the artists, and as fans around the world listen and join in the songs, they form a planetary choir of satanic praise."[18]

Jeff Godwin notes that, "The demons just talk while their Rock and CCM dupes sing."[19] Referring to some examples of his music research, Godwin furthermore points out that there were, "Demonic voices manifest in both forward and reverse modes during LIVE church worship. In one example, a demon voice like that of a young child rails against the preaching. Other manifestations praise Lucifer in reverse even as the church worship team sings normally."[20] Godwin concludes, "Once the doorway is opened, the demons say whatever they wish, regardless of the intent of the human voices."[21]

Jack Wheaton asks, "Have we unknowingly introduced into the sanctuary pagan rhythms, repetitive chanting, and loud emotional performances that are more apt to encourage demonic forces rather than drive them out…?"[22]

With Contemporary Christian music, forms of pagan drumbeat music entered the church. Its unholy influence must not be underestimated. Mickey Hart, drumbeat expert and former percussionist for the *Grateful Dead* rock band, points out that such music will form a union with the spirit world and that, "it is the preferred medium for communication with the gods."[23]

Thus, the church is made a resort for demonic spirits. The Bible pictures the unfaithful end time churches as fallen Babylon, which, "is become the habitation of devils, and the hold of every

---

18   "What's wrong with rock music?" truth.5u.com/rockmusic.html (accessed May 29, 2013); "Today's Music & the Church" http://www.maranathamrc.com/ MHG39%20HOPE.pdf (accessed May 29, 2013).

19   Godwin, *What's Wrong with Christian Rock?* p. 144.

20   Ibid., p. 154.

21   Ibid., p. 155.

22   Wheaton, *Crisis in Christian Music*, p. 23.

23   Mickey Hart and Fredric Liberman, *Spirit into Sound: The Magic of Music*, pp. 179, 184.

foul spirit."[24]

Ellen White warns that, "Satan will make music a snare by the way in which it is conducted."[25] "The *powers* of *satanic* agencies *blend* with the din and noise, to have a carnival, and this is termed the Holy Spirit's working ... No encouragement should be given to this kind of worship."[26]

Contemporary churches that prefer to be modern and up-to-date are usually poor in relation to the holiness of sincere dedication, heartfelt devotion, and true sanctification. While writing about the end-time religion, Ellen White declares, "Their profession, their prayers, and their exhortations are an abomination in the sight of God ... An innumerable host of evil angels are spreading over the whole land and crowding the churches."[27]

---

24   Rev. 18:2
25   Ellen G. White, *Selected Messages*, book 2, p. 38.
26   Ibid., pp. 36, 37, emphasis added.
27   Ellen G. White, *Early Writings*, p. 274.

Chapter 11

More on Demonic Activity

The apostasy in this time of the end appears as a form of great godliness. Few people realize what is going on. They dream of a sweeping revival. However, this is not a revival that glorifies God. It is a false revival led by Satan, and modern Christian music plays a key role.

Perhaps you may not agree, and still think it has been exaggerated to portray modern Christian music as demonic. However, remember research has taken place. Several sources clearly attest that rock music, with contemporary Christian rock inclusive, bears a demonic character.

Scientists, historians, and music experts openly endorse the baneful influence of rock music. A highly qualified musician, Dave Roberts, who writes, arranges, performs and teaches music, wrote in a private paper, "There is no disputing that satanic and occult connections occur in the rock world … this is a spiritual minefield and it is right that you should be concerned that many Christians are ignorant of these matters."[1] He warned naive readers in a Christian music magazine, "I'll bet you aren't aware of all the occultic propaganda in your record collections."[2]

John Makujina indicates that, "the conservative position against rock music has been supported through studies performed by reputable

---

1   Blanchard and Lucarini, *Can We Rock the Gospel?* p. 77.
2   Ibid.

researchers in the social sciences, as well as a blue ribbon panel of historians and musicologists, most of whom have no religious agenda or bias against rock music."[3]

African drummer Stephen Maphosah was trained in demonic worship to instill demon spirits into people. As he became a Christian, he rejected this kind of beat because he realized how damaging it was. On June 25, 1990 he bought samples of ten individual contemporary Christian musicians and groups from a Christian bookstore. He then evaluated this music and recognized the demonic beat, as well as variations that he was accustomed to in his ancestral worship of evil spirits. Without exception, he classified all of the samples as unacceptable and as offensive to Christians.[4]

Another African drummer, Babatunde Olatunji, was just as stunned when he came to America and discovered African rhythms in the music he heard. When expressing his thoughts, he related, "I was so stunned. I remember thinking, hey that's African music; it sounds like what's at home. And the same thing happened when I heard gospel music."[5]

One of Juanita McElwain, professor of music therapy at Florida State University, areas of expertise includes the effects of music on brain waves. She has given many seminars on the effects of music throughout the United States and Europe. Remarkably, McElwain's careful research has endorsed the thoughts of Ellen White on music and its effects, and on how Satan, by certain kinds of music, is able to access and manipulate the human mind.

The belief that music is neutral and without specific influence upon our spiritual welfare, or that it is only a matter of taste or preference, is a great mistake. Throughout all centuries the power and

---

3   Makujina, *Measuring the Music,* p. 249.
4   McElwain, *The Lord is My Song,* p. 93.
5   Mickey Hart, Jay Stevens, and Fredric Lieberman, *Drumming at the Edge of Magic: A Journey into the Spirit of Percussion,* p. 215; cf. Karl Tsatalbasidis, *Drums, Rock, and Worship,* pp. 33, 34.

influence of music has been realized, with or apart from the words.[6] Remember, Satan is very intelligent and knows exactly how to deceive people with music. When we perform or listen to the unholy forms of rock music, regardless of whether it is secular or Christian, demons can take possession of us and dominate our minds.

There is a direct, traceable link between the African demonic voodoo music and all of today's different forms of rock music. Animistic ritual voodoo music was, through the slave trade, brought from Africa to other countries and became the universal platform for popular beat music. David Tame, a widely known American music expert, explains:

> Musicologists and historians are in no doubt that the drum rhythms of Africa were carried to America and were there transmitted and translated into the style of music which became known as jazz. Since jazz and the blues were the parents of rock and roll, this also means that there exists a direct line of descent from the voodoo ceremonies of Africa, through jazz, to rock and roll and all of the other forms of rock music current today.[7]

Thus it is clear that demonic forms of music are at the root of all the modern Western music styles, including Christian rock and gospel music. McElwain, stressing the impact of this by explaining that in various pagan religions, "we find a spirit possession which is echoed, primarily through the beat of the music, in rock music, in faith healing, and in churches of all persuasions, through rock music, Christian rock music, Contemporary Christian music, and country gospel."[8]

She plainly declares that spirit possession in our Christian culture has become very real, "The devil has done a good job of infiltrating our culture, including our Christian culture, with spirit possession, which

---

6   McElwain, *The Lord is My Song,* pp. 41, 42.
7   David Tame, *The Secret Power of Music,* p. 190; cf. David W. Cloud, *Contemporary Christian Music,* pp. 155–160.
8   McElwain, *The Lord is My Song,* p. 70.

may be very real, even though people do not realize that it is happening to them."[9]

Some people may be skeptical about spirit possession through rock music, but McElwain explains:

> Yet it is literally true and a good case can be made for it. If rock music comes from and is inspired by Satan, then it logically follows that those who are involved in it in any way will be affected by Satan and his angels. A number of results will follow including any which are present in any form of demon possession. These may be physical or mental. A person's whole value system may be completely changed. It may be described as conversion. When one is converted to Christ there is a change and he or she becomes a new creature. So too, rock music through demon possession may convert a person to Satan (even unknowingly) and he too will become a 'new creature.'[10]

She also emphasizes that, "It is important to consider how Satan attacks invisibly and imperceptibly through music. This is one of his most terrible counterfeits."[11]

---

9   Ibid.
10   Ibid., pp. 106, 107.
11   Ibid., p. 71.

Chapter 12

Examples

Satan, through music, knows precisely how to gain access to un-suspicious, harmless people.[1] Some practical examples may illustrate the influence of demons through an unholy musical beat. Theodore E. Wade, an American medical doctor who studied hypnotism and similar phenomena for many years, describes the following incident:

SANDY. She was a student at a Christian boarding school who had been secretly listening to rock music records. She suffered severe depression, headaches, frightful nightmares, and couldn't concentrate.

When she listened Satan seemed to be speaking in the background in a horrifying manner. Sandy began to cry and scream. Some people tried to help her, but she pushed them easily aside, and when someone tried to pray she would scream and laugh with a hideously deep voice. The Bible that was given to her was thrown aside. "Someone asked, 'Satan, why don't you get out and leave Sandy alone? She belongs to Jesus.' 'I know she belongs to God and you,' the voice replied, 'but I am going to take all I can get.'" The music record was found and broken and it was then that God answered the prayers for release.

Afterwards, Sandy explained that she heard the people around her, but could only see the devil sitting beside her on the bed. "When

---

1   Read Elaine's experience in which she writes, "As the music is played, these demons are summoned into the room to afflict the person playing the music, and anyone else who is listening" ("A Satanist Testifies About Rock," New Covenant Ministries, http://www.nccg.org/occult/Occult022-Rock2.html [accessed on May 1, 2013]).

the record was broken, she felt release from the power which had controlled her." She joined the others in singing and prayer; clasped her Bible and promised, "I will never let you go again."[2] Pastor Glen Gessele, chaplain of the student body, remarked, "If permitted, Satan is able to slip in and take over a person's mind and body. In Sandy's case, she persistently listened to records which she knew to be forbidden and satanic."[3]

CECIL. Juanita McElwain writes about a member of her family who said that her husband, Cecil, enjoyed listening to popular Christian music. Because she did not appreciate it she banned her husband to a bedroom while he listened to this music.

After some time strange things began to occur. There were odd noises and things began to move unexpectedly. When reading one of Juanita's books she said, "That is the answer. Cecil's music is calling the spirits into our house." When they stopped the music the strange occurrences stopped as well. Initially they were not aware that this kind of music was calling demons into their house.[4]

Such incidents are not to be regarded as extreme or rare. It may happen more often than we think. McElwain writes, "Not only is there documentation of such practices on video and tape, but descriptions are found in the ethno-musicology literature."[5]

JENNIFER. Roger J. Morneau was formerly a Satanist, but has since turned to God and became a Seventh-day Adventist. He described what happened to Kevin and Jennifer, a young married couple from Australia who came to visit him in his home in America. Jennifer lived under very great pressure from several demonic spirits.

The problems started when she attended a rock concert.

2   T.E. Wade, *Spirit Possession,* pp. 55, 56.
3   Ibid., p. 58.
4   McElwain, *The Lord Is My Song,* p. 68.
5   Ibid.

Everything was done to help her. There was much prayer and she was even anointed during a special service. However, in spite of all that was done there was no recovery in any way. One day when Kevin and Jennifer paid Morneau a visit, he discovered that Jennifer had a small cassette player in her shoulder bag that she used to listen to rock music with.

Morneau then relates, "I explained to Kevin that demonic spirits had used the music to take control of his wife's mental and emotional faculties, and intended to drive her to an early grave." Morneau made it clear that Jennifer had to give up this music before she could escape the evil forces. However, that was not very easily or quickly done.

One morning Jennifer was severely attacked and wounded by a demon power. She felt somehow that someone was present when she entered the bathroom. She was thrown down while her head was held and bumped up and down on the floor. Jennifer cried loudly and Kevin came in while this scene was going on. Kevin's prayer, *dear Jesus help*, stopped the attack. This incident convinced Jennifer that Morneau was right and she determined to give up rock music completely. Prayer on her behalf brought the redeeming power of Christ into her life, and before long she was of sound mind and body.[6]

GIANI. Another interesting story is Giani's deliverance from thirty-seven demons as told by Pastor Mario Valente. Giani was born in Brazil and had been demon possessed since her childhood. For two years different treatments were tried unsuccessfully. The various exorcist séances offered at spiritualist centers, different churches, or by witch doctors, were not able to cure Giani. Then a friend, Mrs. Clari, invited Giani's mother to take the girl to an Adventist church. Only when the Biblical rules are practiced with a sincere and dedicated spirit, can healing be possible. When Christ's apostles were unable to cure

6   Roger Morneau, *Beware of Angels,* pp. 35–42.

a young man, possessed with a demon, Christ said, "Howbeit this kind goeth not out but by prayer and fasting."[7]

The Adventist pastor went every night with a team of three persons to Giani's home to pray for her release. The church members were also praying and fasting during this time. The demons did leave her during the following days, but they protested severely. The struggle was intense. It took eighty-eight days to cure her completely. During the process of liberation, the demons taunted and ridiculed the church members, saying that they belonged to them. "The devil would then mention sins such as novel reading, listening to popular music, or wearing make-up, and would say that because the person did not give these up, they belonged to him."[8]

This illustrates something that is in light of this book a great interest. The devil will claim those who are not willing to give up listening to popular music and practicing other unsuspected demonic traps. It also illustrates that real church growth of truly converted people is not advanced in any way by the use of popular music styles, but by giving them up.

Giani was baptized into the Seventh-day Adventist church at Caxias do Sul. The Translator's Postscript, by Harry Bennett, Jr. says: "More than 50 persons have been baptized as a result of Giani's experience. There is not a more consecrated or dedicated church group in this state than the one at Caxias do Sul."[9] Music is a very serious matter. It should be realized that the much-extolled popular Christian music styles may call up demons and dispel the holy angels of God.

---

7   Matt. 17:21.
8   Mario Valente, "The Liberation of Giani," *Review and Herald,* July 4, 1974, p. 20.
9   Ibid.

Chapter 13

Influence and Effects

Music in all of its forms has a certain influence and effect, both physically and spiritually, either for good or for bad. In America, in 1990, a booklet was published about the influence and effects of popular Christian music. Individual testimonies from forty-four young people, ages fifteen to twenty-three, were related. These young people had personally experienced the negative influence and effects of Christian rock.[1]

Some of their complaints were: an addiction to the beat, having undesired thoughts and feelings (unholy, immoral and indecent), and a lack of inner peace.[2] Kimberley Smith, a church musician, tells the story about a Biblical counselor who often meets rebellious young people who at first listened to Contemporary Christian music, but then graduated to heavier forms of rock because the Contemporary Christian music did not satisfy them anymore.

This same counselor was also sought out for help by someone who had a severe sexual addiction that he could not overcome. The person eventually realized the cause of his problem. "He said the trigger for his failure was listening to popular

---

1   Kimberley Smith, *Music and Morals,* p. 71, 72.
2   Ibid.

Christian music. Whether in Church or in the car, this music would stir a strong desire to fulfil the lust."[3]

Smith concludes, "This is not an unusual circumstance, and I would say immoral thoughts, triggered by the sensual sound and delivery techniques of CCM, are common in our churches."[4]

Wheaton adds the following sobering words to this revelation:

> Certain rhythms will instantly attract demonic forces, trigger aggressive behaviour, and destroy moral codes and any sense of modesty or self-control … We have left the door open in our sanctuaries, evangelical rallies, and youth meetings to the evil forces of Satan through the tribal, demonically-inspired rhythms … If you feel more like 'moving, swaying, clapping' … it is dangerous … Be aware that rhythm is the most sensitive and the most powerful tool for demonic forces to invade church music … The hypnotic spell cast by repetitive rhythms, layered and repeated over and over, has crept into Christian music.[5]

Many Christians seriously underestimate the influences and effects of music. Frank Garlock and Kurt Woetzel are both music teachers of the *Majesty Music* staff in the Choral Seminars, which reaches an average of over 700 church musicians each year. In these seminars it is taught how the Bible applies to music. They also show Christians what is wrong with contemporary music and provide a replacement for it. That replacement took the form of *Majesty Music Inc.,* the largest independent recording and publishing company for Bible-believing Christians. Garlock and Woetzel explain that there are many knowledgeable writers and experts in the fields of the psychology of music, the philosophy of music, and the sociology of music, who are without any Christian background or experience. "Yet

3   Ibid.
4   Ibid., p. 72.
5   Wheaton, *Crisis in Christian Music,* pp. 59, 66, 68, 78.

they perceive the issue of music and communication better, from a social and psychological perspective, than many Christians who have a spiritual viewpoint."[6]

It has also been clearly demonstrated that certain sound waves can have a deadly effect. Research has shown that plants grow well under the sound of classical music, but that they gradually die off when they are exposed to rock music.[7]

Wheaton warns that low frequency vibrations, such as bass and drum sounds, can cause extensive damage to the human body and mind if not kept below the 90-decibel level. He describes how one scientist was killed when he hooked up a whistle to a compressed air machine and decided to stay in the testing laboratory while his assistant turned on the air compressor. The powerful low frequencies and the decibel level of the sound killed the unfortunate scientist. The autopsy revealed that his, "internal organs had literally been 'scrambled' by the power of the soundwaves."[8]

There is also evidence that low frequency sound waves produced on sea by air guns cause severe damage to marine life:

> A new study says low-frequency sounds from human activities can affect squid and other cephalopods, not just whales and other marine mammals, which have long been thought to be vulnerable to such pulses … In the early 2000s the remains of giant squid were found off Spain's Asturias province. In each case, the creatures' bodies appeared soon after ships had used air guns to conduct low-frequency sound-pulse exercises in the region, in some cases for oil-and-gas prospecting efforts. Scientists investigating the giant squid remains at the time found

6   Frank Garlock and Kurt Woetzel, *Music in the Balance,* p. 33.

7   Tame, *The Secret Power of Music,* p. 143; Wheaton, *Crisis in Christian Music,* pp. 26, 27.

8   Wheaton, *Crisis in Christian Music,* p. 26; cf. McElwain, *The Lord is My Song,* pp. 131, 132.

evidence of extensive bodily damage, including mantles reduced to pulp, bruised muscles, and lesions in statocysts. These fluid-filled organs rest behind the creatures' eyes and help giant squid maintain balance and position. 'With this study, we now have proof that low-frequency sounds can harm cephalopods,' said Guerra, a marine biologist at Spain's Marine Research Institute.[9]

In *Citizen Link,* an email newsletter from a family advocacy organization that inspires men and women to live out biblical citizenship that transform culture, it was reported on June 28, 2002, that the *National Coalition for the Protection of Children and Families* had talked with teenagers who attended *rave* parties—dance parties that last the whole night. The effects of the music and dance were such that these youngsters said that it was like having sex with your clothes on.[10]

David Tame explains:

> The effect of jazz syncopation is primarily sexual: the beat somehow ties in with the rhythm of sexuality in man and woman. In fact, hard, loud, relentless pulsation also has a similar effect ... increasing the outpouring into the bloodstream of sexual hormones ... It is not unknown for those who are the chief producers of these rhythms, the drummers of modern music, to actually have music-induced orgasms after several hours of non-stop drumming.[11]

The argument that music is neutral can by no means in any way be verified. Jeff Godwin, a former slave to Rock music who completely transformed his life and started a ministry of researching and exposing the evils in Rock music, states, "Enough evidence now exists to clearly show that when rock is played, our bodies, minds and spirits suffer."[12]

9   Ker Than, *National Geographic News,* May 3, 2011.
10   McElwain, *The Lord is My Song,* p. 132.
11   Tame, *The Secret Power of Music,* p. 199.
12   Godwin, *Dancing with Demons,* p. 11.

He continues:

> Rock music has also been found to cause chemical imbalances in the human body. The bass tones and driving drumbeats of modern rock have been proven to demonstrate a reaction with the cerebral-spinal fluid and pituitary gland of the brain. When exposed to rock, the adrenaline and sex glands over-secrete. Their hormonal production is pushed into over-drive. This is why concert-going crowds 'bang their heads,' raise their fists and destroy the arena. It's also why feelings of lust and sensuality wash over everyone there.[13]

As to the uncontrollable behavioral reaction to music, Wheaton points out:

> Because music enters the mid-brain, you cannot censor your body's reaction to music … This is why music is so powerful. It is capable of seizing control of the individual, overpowering the higher senses of reason and logic in the hypothalamus, and cause people to do things their higher brain would object to. That's why I believe music can be used as a drug, and it is probably the most dangerous drug we have on the market today.[14]

Some may think that Contemporary Christian music is different and not comparable to secular music because the rhythm is often not that strong. They feel a good case can be made by asking, "If there is only a soft beat or a much subdued rock rhythm, how then can that ever cause any harm?" Many Christians seem to feel flattered and very comfortable with this thought. How misleading this idea is!

Consider what Juanita McElwain, an expert in this field of music,

---

13   Ibid.; cf. Blanchard and Lucarini, *Can We Rock the Gospel,* p. 137.

14   Wheaton, *Crisis in Christian Music,* p. 93.

has to say, "The rock beats (in CCM) are often so subdued that the listener actually reports the music to be sedative, whereas in fact objective measurement shows the subdued rock beat has the same psycho-physiological effects as that of harder rock."[15]

She continues:

> In sensual music, in addition or instead of the toe-tap-ping there is a swaying induced. Be careful, if the music makes you feel like swaying or if you see people around you swaying. Hypnotic effects may be produced by many repetitions, short phrases, small melodic range without large jumps. Examples of this may be seen in so-called Celebration music. After prolonged hearing *it is possible for this to lead to a trance-like state.* The abundant use of certain notes and chords, such as blue notes, 6th chords, major 7th chords, diminished 7th chords and chromaticism produce sensual feelings ... One of the biggest sources of the sensual music in our churches is what is called Contemporary Christian music.[16]

Explaining why modern Christian music is not appropriate in church, Wheaton observes with clear words:

> The most *natural* thing you want to do when listening ... to contemporary Christian music songs when played with a rock beat ... is to *move your body*, snap your fingers, clap your hands, wiggle your hips, stomp your feet—*it is dance music and it is designed to produce this effect.* That's why older people in church are confused; they came to worship, not dance ... It is the *antithesis* of why they go to church. It's also very characteristic of the described musical styles accompanying

---

15   McElwain, *The Lord is My Song*, p. 125, emphasis added.
16   Ibid., emphasis added.

pagan religions popular at the time of Christ and the development of the early church. The early church fathers kept telling Christians to *come out* of the world system. I don't think this means to sneak the world system's musical styles into the church.[17]

Popular Christian music in church is not harmless. The undesirable physical effects it may induce are a very real and common phenomenon that should not be taken lightly. It is further attested by Wheaton:

> Low register musical vibrations carry farther and have more power than any other register. They also can affect internal organs and the endocrine gland system. The often insensitive use of the electric bass in church praise bands can be producing a physical response, particularly among the young, that is often in direct contradiction to the feelings of awe, respect and love that we are trying for when we worship our Lord and Saviour. One of the most constant abuses I hear with praise bands is in this area.[18]

Remember, however, that it is also a demonstrated fact that sanctified music has a beneficial and curative effect, both physically and spiritually. Only this kind of music is appropriate to praise and worship God with. When David played on his harp, the evil spirit that troubled King Saul was calmed.[19] David feared God. He played sacred music that was, "lofty and Heaven-inspired."[20]

However, imagine if David would have played rock music with a band. Do you think that Saul would have been refreshed? Oh, certainly not. Without a doubt the demonic harassment in his life would have become worse.

---

17 Wheaton, *Crisis in Christian Music*, p. 87, emphasis original.
18 Ibid., p. 83.
19 1 Sam. 16:14–23
20 Ellen G. White, *Signs of the Times*, August 3, 1888, p. 234.

Chapter 14

Brain Waves

Our whole body is regulated by rhythm. Mickey Hart, a specialist in the field of rhythm, notes:

> Within the body itself the main rhythm is laid down by the cardiovascular system, the heart and the lungs, the heart beating between sixty to eighty times per minute, the lungs filling and emptying at about a quarter that speed. But again these are only the most obvious bodily rhythms. From the vibration of single cells to the slow peristalsis of our intestines, our internal machinery is all moving in a complex dance whose synchronization is carefully monitored by the central nervous system, which then reports on the state of our internal rhythms to the midbrain.[1]

It is common knowledge that our brains produce signals, vibrations, microwaves, and brain waves, all of which can be measured. They are rendered in Hertz according to vibrations or cycles per second (cps). The neurons of the brain are constantly firing waves or vibrations that are called, *neuro chemical cortical brain activity*.

According to their frequency, brain waves are usually divided into four main groups, also referred to as *brain states*:

1. The fully awake and alert *Beta* state ranges from about 14–40

---

1   Hart, Stevens, and Lieberman, *Drumming at the Edge of Magic: A Journey into the Spirit of Percussion*, p. 121.

cps and is associated with activity of the left brain or conscious mind.

2. The relaxed *Alpha* state ranges from about 8–13 cps and is associated with right brain activity or the subconscious mind.
3. The deeply relaxed *Theta* state ranges from about 4–7 cps and is associated with the right brain or deep subconscious mind.
4. The unconscious *Delta* state ranges from about 0.5–3.5 cps and is associated with no thinking and has access to nonphysical states of existence.

Generally, in the awake *Beta* state, the attention is focused outward. In *Alpha* it begins to turn inward and as the brainwave frequencies decrease, it goes further and further inward.

At the borderline between the brain states *Beta* and *Alpha* is a doorway to the subconscious mind. Hypnotherapy, intended as a process of strengthening the effect of mind over body, focuses on entering this doorway to embed messages into the subconscious mind. These messages are called *subliminals,* and refer to the information received below the level of conscious awareness. Subliminals by-pass the conscious mind and go directly to the subconscious.

Hypnosis is also a tool that is used effectively by the forces of darkness, usually without the awareness of those who practice it and those who are hypnotized. It is very important to realize that Satan has a thorough knowledge of the workings of the human brain. Ellen White points out that Satan, for some thousands of years, "has been experimenting upon the properties of the human mind, and he has learned to know it well." [2]

Watch carefully how Satan works and precisely what he does to bring human beings under his influence:

> By his subtle workings in these last days *he is linking the human mind with his own, imbuing it with his thoughts*; and he is doing this work in so deceptive a manner that

---

2   Ellen G. White, *Medical Ministry,* p. 111.

those who accept his guidance know not that they are being led by him at his will. The great deceiver hopes so to confuse the minds of men and women that none but his voice will be heard.[3]

How can Satan link the human mind with his own and imbue it with his thoughts? It has a great deal to do with natural laws and the frequency of the brain waves. To understand this process, remember this basic principle: Only when the emitter and receiver have the same frequency is communication possible. Two similar tuning forks may illustrate this. When you strike one of them, it is interesting to note that the sound produced will spontaneously cause the other fork to vibrate and produce the same sound as well.

This sympathetic or co-operative resonance could occur because both forks have a similar vibrational pattern, with a similar frequency, which made communication possible. In other words, it allowed a spontaneous energy transfer from the one fork to the other.

Another important related principle of nature is the law of entrainment, which works with both animate and inanimate objects. This rule was first discovered by the Dutch scientist Christiaan Huygens. When Christiaan placed two clocks close to each other he found that they would eventually end up ticking synchronously.

Thus we have these two natural principles that go together and play an important role in our everyday living:

1. The principle of spontaneous communication—the transfer of a message or of energy.
2. The principle of spontaneous entrainment—the ability to adjust and come in tune with impulses of another source.

Music therapy is based on these two natural principles and can have a powerful effect in correcting and restoring a healthy balance. The whole human body, including all of our organs, glands, cells, molecules and atoms, vibrate at a fundamental frequency of approximately eight

3   Ibid., emphasis added.

cycles per second. The vibrational frequencies of the different organs in our body are able to entrain to each other in order to maintain harmony.

Jonathan S. Goldman is a specialist in sound healing. He is the founder and director of *Sound Healers Associations Inc.* and president of *Spirit Music, Inc.,* which produces music for meditation, self-healing, and transformation. He explains:

> As the functions of the human body can entrain to each other, it is possible to use external rhythms to affect the internal mechanism of heart rate, respiration and brain wave activity. This ability to affect internal rhythms by external means seems fairly logical and matter of fact. Yet research into this area did not make its way into scientific journals until the 1970s, when studies began to report that resonance and entrainment of bodily processes can occur in response to external sound and musical rhythms.[4]

It has been demonstrated that sound frequencies affect body frequencies both positively and negatively. Wheaton notes, "musical vibrations that are in tune with our human vibratory pattern could have a profound healing effect on the entire body"[5] He also stated, "The brain tries to speed up our pulse rate to where it more closely matches that of the music."[6] So in music therapy, music frequencies are used to affect body rhythms, heart rate, blood pressure, muscle electrical activity, etc. All of this is based on the principle of entrainment.

Jonathan Goldman explains further:

> Entrainment is an aspect of sound that is closely related to rhythms and the way these rhythms affect us. It is a phenomenon of sound in which the powerful rhythmic vibrations of one object will cause the less powerful vibrations

---

4   Jonathan S. Goldman, *Music Physician for Times to Come,* p. 221.
5   Wheaton, *Crisis in Christian Music,* p. 90
6   Ibid., p. 61

of another object to lock in step and oscillate at the first object's rate … With entrainment you are changing the natural oscillatory patterns of one object and replace them with the different oscillatory patterns of another object … Entrainment is found throughout nature. Fireflies blinking on and off entrain with each other … Muscle cells from the heart, when they move closer together, suddenly shift in their rhythm and start pulsing together, perfectly synchronized.[7]

Since each level of consciousness of the human brain is characterized by a particular vibration frequency, it is possible to affect these levels or link up with them when the particular corresponding sound frequency is produced and often repeated.[8]

Tibetan meditation bells produce a sound frequency in the form of brain waves that prepare the mind for meditation. The sound will make the brain shift to the frequency of the aimed level of consciousness:

An examination reveals that the two bells, which are rung together, are slightly out of tune with each other. Depending upon the bells, the different tones between them create ELFs [extremely low frequencies] somewhere between 4 and 8 cycles per second. This falls exactly within the range of the brain waves created during meditation and helps shift the brain to these frequencies.[9]

Thus, speaking of jazz syncopation, Tame explained a similar shift that, "the beat somehow ties in with the rhythm of sexuality in man and woman."[10] Sexuality is a gift from God and a blessing to humanity if properly practiced within a marriage relationship. Satan has made music as well as sex a successful snare to derail his victims, bringing

---

7   Jonathan S. Goldman, *Music Physician for Times to Come,* pp. 218–220.
8   Cf. Peter Michael Hamel, *Through Music to the Self*, p. 108.
9   Goldman, *Music Physician for Times to Come,* pp. 228, 229.
10   Tame, *The Secret Power of Music,* p. 199.

misfortune on them and perverting the human that were created in God's image.

Robert Monroe, director of the Mutual Broadcasting System in the southeast of the USA, had several out-of-body experiences. Because of this he started private research into the effects of different frequencies on various states of consciousness.

> Part of Monroe's experience with out-of-body travels involved hearing different frequencies which he felt triggered the experiences. He felt that sound somehow could play a role in helping others achieve similar states of consciousness, and with the help of a research team, he set out to discover if he could control or drive the brain with sound waves. Through trial and error and probably a lot of intuition, Monroe discovered that specific frequencies could produce entrainment of brain waves. He found that, much like a glass resonated by a pure tone, the brain resonated when bombarded with pulsing sound waves … The frequencies Monroe used to entrain the brain were in the same spectrum as the brain waves themselves—from 5 hz to about 20 hz. These are frequencies that the human ear is incapable of hearing.[11]

Satan knows the laws of nature better than we do and he utilizes all possible means to control the human mind to advance his cause. The use of different sound frequencies to achieve experiences of consciousness outside of the body is another device of Satan that he uses to entrap humans. It confuses the mind as to what is truth, so that people believe that man is immortal and that forms of life and consciousness are possible apart from the body. Such devices are based on the great lie of Satan, "Ye shall not surely die."[12] With the rhythmic pulsing sound

---

11   Goldman, *Music Physician for Times to Come,* p. 223.
12   Gen. 3:4.

waves of rock music, Satan can influence and adjust the frequency of the brain waves to bring them in tune with himself in order to link the human mind with his own.

Chapter 15

Far Reaching Results

Different kinds of music have the ability to affect different changes in human behavior, emotions, and physiology. Since much music is nonverbal in its nature, and if not performed in its extreme forms, it usually meets little intellectual resistance. The sound of music has its primary effect on the right part of the brain. Verbal messages appeal more directly to logic and initiate its action, activating the left part of the brain. Music therefore, tends to 'pass' the brain without activating the reasoning abilities, which makes its influence subtler and its appeal to a wider and greater character.

The influence of music primarily affects the mind, which activates the body and initiates a response that may create a different balance of body, mind, and spirit. Alfred A. Tomatis, a French ear specialist and pioneer in sound therapy treatment, notes, "that the brain receives more stimuli from the ears than from any other organ."[1] The impact on our brain when listening to music should not be underestimated.

It is beyond question that music exerts a profound effect on the entire human body. It is a demonstrated fact that music makes it possible to influence and adjust body rhythms, including the frequency of the human brain waves, either for good or for bad. Depending upon the kind of music, its effect may be energizing or nerve shattering, exciting or calming, distracting or focusing, pleasing or irritating, uplifting or degrading, healing or harming. The influence of music is by no means neutral. Music can have far reaching results and bring about a

---

1   Don Campbell, ed., *Music: Physician for Times to Come*, p. 45.

total change in the human life. The influence of music on the mind, body, and spirit can be very drastic and impressive.

When the sound of music has the right frequency even a small particle like the atom can be changed. Cathie E. Guzzetta, director of the Holistic Nursing Consultants in Bethesda, Maryland, explains that, "it is possible that musical vibrations that are in tune with our fundamental vibratory pattern could have a profound healing effect on the entire human body and mind, affecting changes in emotions and in organs, enzymes, hormones, cells, and atoms."[2]

Of particular interest and great importance, is the truth that music can bring about altered states of consciousness. "When appropriately applied, music can be a way of reaching nonordinary levels of human consciousness. One is able to pass from ordinary states of consciousness to an altered state of consciousness to achieve the mind's fullest potential."[3]

Note the various effects that certain music passages can have:

> Music elicits a variety of different experiences in individuals. During relaxation and music therapy, clients reaching an altered state of consciousness may visualize settings, peaceful scenes, images, or may experience various sensations or moods. Music passages can evoke scenes from fantasy to real life. Melodic patterns can evoke love, joy, and deep peace.[4]

If melodic patterns of music can evoke such positive results, what then might be the result when rock patterns are played with pulsing drum sounds?

Alfred Tomatis explains:

> The low frequency, percussive sounds cause exaggerated

---

2   Ibid., p. 155.

3   Ibid., p. 152.

4   Ibid., p. 155; cf. Helen Bonny and Louis Savary, *Music and Your Mind,* p. 30.

movement of the endolymphatic liquid which begins to move, just as it would in an elevator starting up. If this movement is too continuous, the subject loses the image of his body and enters into a kind of hypnosis. Very few are able to resist moving to the beat of a drum. It puts us at the mercy of the drummer, a magus who can then do with his listeners whatever he wants.[5]

Satan has made music a snare. He knows how to use the right sound of frequencies to make the human brain shift to the frequencies that allow him to imbue his secret messages and thoughts into our minds. The only possible way of escaping his snares is to avoid all forms of rock music and to seek out divine protection by living a dedicated, faithful Christian life.

---

5   Campbell, *Music: Physician for Times to Come*, p. 23.

Chapter 16

Subliminal Messages

As noted earlier, it has been discovered that certain sound frequencies can affect and entrain brain waves when they are of the same spectrum from about 9 Hz to 20 Hz. Vibrations or sound waves in this range are inaudible to the human ear. This spectrum provides a gate to the subconscious. Inaudible messages within this spectrum can be stored imperceptibly as subliminals in the subconscious.

Cathie E. Guzzetta explains, "The subliminal technique delivers verbal messages to the individual at a volume so low or through a change in speed or frequency so fast that the conscious mind cannot perceive it. The conscious mind responds to the music while the unconscious mind absorbs and responds to the verbal suggestion."[1] Thus, any kind of message may enter the brain easily without us realizing its character because the conscious mind is in fact by-passed.

Professor Wilson Bryan Key, a Californian specialist and pioneer in this area, explains, "Likewise, auditory perception at the conscious level is limited to a finite range of sound, volume, and tonal frequency levels; beyond these ranges are frequencies where information can be transmitted invisibly into the unconscious."[2]

The *Love Tapes Catalog* presents a variety of meditation and subliminal scripture tapes with silent commands buried deep under layers of nature sounds that are supposed to help people learn the Word and grow in Christ. This catalog explains:

---

1   Campbell, *Music: Physician for Times to Come,* p. 157; cf. Steven Halpern and Louis Savary, *Sound Health,* p. 137.
2   Wilson Bryan Key, *Subliminal Seduction,* p. 26, 27.

> Subliminal messages are undetectable by the outer mind, yet easily picked up by the inner mind which influences many of our actions, habits abilities, likes and dislikes … You should play the tapes as often as possible but there is no need to 'consciously' listen to them. You simply turn on the tape and hear gentle ocean waves or music while you receive the desired messages without resistance from your outer mind.[3]

The unbiblical rather popular concept of not investigating anything[4] seems to be, *Don't question—just listen.* The real danger of listening to subliminal messages is that they are received unknowingly, without resistance, and we do not consciously realize the effect they may have.

Rock musicians are usually well aware of this process. The late Jimi Hendrix, one of the greatest rock guitarists of all time, addressed this similar phenomenon. He put it in these words: "Atmospheres are going to come through music, because music is a spiritual thing of its own. You can hypnotize people with music, and when you get people at the weakest point, you can preach to them into the subconscious what we want to say … The music flows from the air; that's why I connect with a spirit."[5]

Note that Jimi Hendrix states that the music flows from the air and that he connects with a spirit.[6] This means that there is a demon power participating in the rock music performance. Hendrix explained that what they want to say is preached into the subconscious.

Thus it is made clear that a demonic power is present to subliminally brainwash people through rock music. This is a real

---

3   Godwin, *What's Wrong with Christian Rock?* p. 131.
4   When it sounds good, feels good, and tastes good, it should be all right.
5   Peters, Peters, and Merrill, *Rock's Hidden Persuader,* p. 81; cf. Godwin, *What's Wrong with Christian Rock,* p. 135.
6   The Bible speaks about the prince of the power of the air, the spirit that is now working in the children of disobedience. Instead of teaming up with a wicked spirit we are to wrestle against these demonic spiritual powers in the air or in the heavenly places. Eph. 2:2; 6:12.

process. The effectiveness of subliminal messages has been scientifically demonstrated.

Wallace LaBenne, psychology professor and psychotherapist, reported that there are a host of studies verifying the effectiveness of subliminal messages. He explains:

> What we know today is that the brain sees and hears more than the eyes and ears. What we further know is it takes certain frequencies of light and sound for the conscious (mind) to pick it up. We want to bypass the censorship of the left brain (the evaluative and rational side) and go to the right brain (which controls attitudes and habits).[7]

This is the kind of unchecked path subliminal messages follow. Satan likes to have his messages passed this way, unnoticed, to the right brain. Research has verified the responses to these stimuli may result in behavior modification. Howard Shevrin, psychologist and expert in subliminal technique research at the University of Michigan, "has been probing electronic responses to subliminal stimulation and has discovered brain-wave 'correlates' that show the brain responding 'differentially' to subliminal messages."[8]

In other words, Shevrin discovered electronic impulses registering unique responses to messages that were unconsciously received. Dependent upon the nature of the received subliminals, these hidden messages can result in a change of behavior, either for good or for bad. This process is usually a form of hypnotic manipulation. This is exactly what Satan does with the sound waves of modern rock, Christian rock, and New Age music.

Research revealed that Christian rock has backmasked messages and subliminals, aimed at the subconscious. McElwain confirms, "There are hidden messages of backward masking and subliminal

---

7   Peters, Peters, and Merrill, *Rock's Hidden Persuader,* p. 33.
8   Peters, Peters, and Merrill, *Rock's Hidden Persuader,* p. 67.

messages in rock music."[9] Thus, through Christian rock, Satan knows how to mislead people in the church in a crafty and cunning way.

McElwain made clear that subliminals are usually used with New Age music.[10] The origin of New Age music dates from the 1970s when, without a clear identity, a new international musical movement emerged. In 1986 the name New Age music was adopted. It carried a wide variety of contemporary, experimental, and traditional styles under its umbrella. New Age music may also include Rock characteristics, such as its typical beat. Compared with Rock it is usually a more refined style of music with mystical, meditative, and transcendental aspects.

Popular themes in New Age music include space and the cosmos, environment and nature, spirituality, wellness in being, harmony with one's self and the world, and dreams and journeys of the mind or spirit. New Age music is in general more appealing to grown up and elderly people.

Popular themes of Rock music include political activism and changes in social attitudes towards race, sex, and drug use. Rock music is in general more attractive and appealing to the youth and is often labeled as an expression of youth revolt against adult consumerism and conformity.

Since a mixtures of music styles are played it is not always possible to clearly classify the kind of music performed. Many modern revival songs are New Age oriented. This is not surprising because Satan, as an angel of light, tries to get all people under his control.

Ellen White warns, "If permitted, the evil angels will work (captivate and control) the minds of men until they have no mind or will of their own."[11] This really is a horrifying and very sad process. We need to be extremely cautious and watchful. We must avoid every possible approach of demonic infiltration. All possible forms of unholy music,

9   McElwain, *The Lord is My Song*, p. 106.
10   Ibid., p. 83.
11   Ellen G. White, *Mind, Character, and Personality*, vol. 1, p. 24.

including Contemporary Christian music, should be consequently eliminated from our homes and churches.

The modern forms of music mask this demonic infiltration process by a most successful and effective means. Satan cunningly employs these methods without the great majority of people realizing what is really going on. Through the secret messages hidden in popular music Satan tries to infiltrate, manipulate and rule the human mind, thus influencing people's actions and behavior.

The words and thoughts that pass through our minds make up for our actions and attitudes. The sum total of all our thoughts, ideas, beliefs, attitudes, and actions determine what kind of person we are and what we live for. The way we think is a fundamental qualifying principle of our being.

The Bible says, "be ye transformed by the renewing of your mind."[12] On the one hand this means that if we live a wrong life and desire a transformation or change for the better, the only possible way is for us to adjust to another way of thinking—a *renewing* of the mind—more positive, noble, and spiritual. On the other hand, when we serve God, Satan knows very well that the only way to transform people to serve him will also be a change of mind—a "renewing" of the mind in his favor. Therefore he tries to influence the human mind in all possible ways to effect a change of thinking that will suit his purpose.

We are in our daily life constantly bombarded with impulses, both good and bad. As mentioned earlier, the brain has two centers. One is a conscious part where we are aware of the incoming impulses that enable us directly to reason, judge, and decide upon them. The other part of the brain, the unconscious subliminal part, is like a storehouse where subliminal impulses, without us knowing or realizing, are received and stored up. Inconspicuous drawings hidden in pictures or undetectably spoken messages embedded in sounds or in music[13] may be stored up in the unconscious mind.

Subliminal messages can play an important part in our life when a situation turns up that is in some way related to a stored subliminal message. The message can then become conscious and possibly serve its intended purpose. Thus a variety of subliminal impulses or messages, such as commercials advertising a certain product, health messages to cure the sick, or messages that are aimed at changing behavior, may be presented in TV spots, pictures, magazines, tapes and records to serve a certain desired goal because evidence shows that it works.

Thus, in a similar way Satan makes use of the backmasking phenomenon in music. There are for instance, hidden messages in Rock music about using drugs. Suppose while listening to music, your unconscious mind picks up the secret message: *Try marijuana, it makes you feel happy.* When in your life a situation arises where you feel miserable because everything seems to be against you, and when you happen to have a friend who uses marijuana, this stored message may emerge into consciousness and keep running through your mind. While you are eagerly longing to feel happy, you will be tempted to seek this friend's company and try *marijuana.* In similar ways many young people and adults are lured into the snares of Satan and are brought under his influence and control. This undoubtedly is why Satan inserts subliminal backward messages in music.

Despite Satan's misleading temptations, we need not be despairing or discouraged. The good news is that we are not a helpless prey. When we take a firm stand on God's side we can conquer him and force his departure.

There is an old saying that says, "We cannot prevent the birds flying above our head but we can prevent that they build a nest upon our head." This makes sense. We can't help that temptations and bad influences come our way, but we can prevent them from taking hold of

---

13   These are not backward messages.

us. Satan can never compel us to do evil. He cannot control the human mind unless it is yielded to him. Our will is decisive and must consent. The secret to living a victorious life and resisting Satan's power and temptations is submission and faith in God, prayer and study of His powerful Word, obedience to His will, and trust in His sure promises. We may even force Satan to flee from us by claiming God's wonderful promises. The Bible says, "Submit yourself therefore to God. Resist the devil, and he will flee from you. Draw nigh to God, and He will draw nigh to you."[14] We cannot conquer Satan's power in our own strength but we are assured,, "The name of the Lord is a strong tower: the righteous runneth into it, and is safe." [15]

Satan trembles and flees even before the weakest soul who finds a hiding place in God's mighty name.

God's holy Word is like His name, powerful enough to prevent anyone from sinning. "Thy word have I hid in my heart, that I might not sin against thee."[16] Just like when Christ conquered Satan's temptations while He was on earth in human form by citing Scripture, "It is written,"[17] so we may also conquer Satan's temptations and false assertions. We have the assurance that God is able to keep us from falling, "Now unto him that is able to keep you from falling, and to present you faultless before the presence of his glory with exceeding joy."[18] As we face temptations, we should keep in mind, "but God is faithful, who will not suffer you to be tempted above that ye are able; but will with the temptation also make a way to escape, that ye may be able to bear it."[19] What a treasure of wonderful promises and infinite love God gives to all those who choose to follow Him, conquer Satan's temptations in His name, and to live a victorious life.

The outcome of rock music is very serious. It is a subculture,

---

14   James 4:7, 8
15   Prov. 18:10
16   Ps. 119:11
17   Matt. 4:4, 7, 10
18   Jude 1:24
19   1 Cor. 10:13

obsessed with rebellion, violent behavior, drugs, alcohol, sex, death, and demonism. These are revealed not only on a worldly level, but in Christian rock music as well. By recognizing the dangers and results of rock music we have a responsibility to warn other people of the bad consequences that follow from listening to it. When a church is not very spiritually minded and there are young people who lack principles and are violent and rebellious, then we should consider if a link with unholy music is the cause.

Chapter 17

Critical Problem

David Tame, a widely known American researcher and musicologist, writes:

> More than any other form of the misuse of sound, it is rock with which we must deal today. There is no question but that rock is intimately related to the kind of state of consciousness found in vast numbers of young people ... Rock has unquestionably affected the philosophy and lifestyle of millions ... Its effect upon the soul is to make nigh-impossible the true inner silence and peace necessary for the contemplation of eternal verities. Its 'fans' are addicted, though they know it not, to the 'feelgood', ego-centricity-enhancing, para-hypnotic effects of its insistent beat. How necessary it is in this age for some to have the courage to be the ones who are 'different', and to separate themselves out from the pack who long ago sold their lives and personalities to this sound and the ... culture which has sprung up around it! I adamantly believe that rock in *all* of its forms is a critical problem which our civilization *must* get to grips with in some genuinely effective way, and without delay, if it wishes long to survive.[1]

Dan and Steve Peters point out the task Christians have to fulfill in this world:

---

1   Tame, *The Secret Power of Music,* p. 204, emphasis original.

> We as Christians have a responsibility to check in every way possible the corruption of our society by whatever means, and that includes subliminal seduction ... But too often we Christians hide behind ... a 'back to the fort' mentality—just hanging on until Jesus comes. Never mind that people are outside the fort, dying for lack of wisdom ... Edmond Burke once said, 'The only thing necessary for the triumph of evil is for good men to do nothing'... we need to stand up and be counted; furthermore, we need to be willing to inform others.[2]

In spite of the fact that the church understands its calling, discerns the dangers, and knows how to counteract them, it often adds its part to the process of misleading by introducing Christian rock and other modern styles of music. Kimberly Smith aptly remarks:

> We have enough troubles trying to stay the course in our Christian lives, why add the negative influence of immoral music, Christian or otherwise? And why promote such music in church where we go to seek refuge from the world and its temptations, as well as for spiritual edification? *Why are we contributing to people's moral failures within the Church?*[3]

The newspaper, *Kansas City Star,* stated that in four "Bible Belt" states, Tennessee, Arkansas, Alabama, and Oklahoma, "the divorce rates ... are about 50 percent above the national average."[4]

Note that Wheaton observed a direct link with the modern music styles in the church:

> Apparently the 'holiness' of God and the sanctity of marriage have both failed in four of the most Christian

---

2   Peters, Peters, and Merrill, *Rock's Hidden Persuader,* pp. 93, 94.

3   Smith, *Music and Morals,* p. 73, emphasis original.

4   Wheaton, *Crisis in Christian Music,* p. 97.

fundamentalist states … What has this to do with music in the church? A lot. I believe that there is no longer a place, with few exceptions, where people can go and experience this holiness. I also believe that the turning to worldly musical styles, with the rational that it will more likely attract the unsaved and keep the young people happy, has failed … it has lowered the standards of holiness as expressed through music and worship.[5]

Ivor Myers, once part of the hip-hop group *The Boogie Monsters*, but now active in evangelism as a Seventh-day Adventist, correctly states:

Without question, the hip-hop and rock cultures are opposed to God's values. The music is an inseparable part of the sinful culture of contemporary society. When music groups try to use Christian words of truth while still clinging to the culture of hip-hop and rock, they are engaged in a mockery of God … The truth is that without a living connection with Christ that produces a fruitful life, our words are of no value, even if they are words of truth. If we do not understand what it means to come out of the world and its ways, we are in constant danger of making a mockery of God and the Christian faith.[6]

Wheaton's experience is that most teenagers are turned off by the musical presentations in the churches, rather than turned on. He explains:

Many people today are trying to *escape* the world, to find a place with peace, love, serenity, and dignity. Where better to go than the church. When they walk in looking for those attributes, and instead are hit in the eyes and ears

---

5   Ibid., p. 98.
6   Ivor Myers, *Escape the Black Hole*, p. 87.

with a poorly rehearsed imitative rock concert (with 'Christian' lyrics) they often walk right back out again, terribly disillusioned.[7]

In his summary, Wheaton states:

> The church used to be a sanctuary; a place where you could escape the franticness, the torment, the sensuality of the world. Sadly, in many churches today, that is no longer the case. Has the world taken over the church?… Have we carelessly and heartlessly dumped over three hundred years of sacred music in the ash-can of history … for the sake of reaching the lost?[8]

Having exposed the serious ill effects of popular music, Wheaton summarizes:

> As shocking as these discoveries are, it is even more shocking to see this music being welcomed with open arms into the sanctuaries of our churches. Have we lost our minds? Are we so divorced from understanding spiritual warfare that we cannot understand that Satan wants to undermine and compromise our worship? Have we so given in to society and our teenagers that we look the other way while evil slithers into our churches—all because we want to attract more teenagers and worldly non-believers?[9]

In our worship services we want to praise and glorify God instead of pleasing and satisfying humans. In church we enter into God's holy presence and when we "select music that was not conceived, inspired, and birthed through a deep respect for the holiness of God we have sought worldly approval rather than spiritual. Whenever the style, the lyric, the melody, and the presentation does not make the performer

---

7   Wheaton, *Crisis in Christian Music,* p. 23, emphasis original.
8   Ibid.
9   Ibid., p. 37.

or the congregation more aware rather than less of the overpowering holiness of God, we have failed in our mission."[10]

Ellen White clearly points out the elevated purpose music should have in worship. She also indicates what the results will be when this high purpose is neglected and a wrong use of music is made:

> Music was made to serve a holy purpose, to lift the thoughts to that which is pure, noble, and elevating, and to awaken in the soul devotion and gratitude to God. What a contrast between the ancient custom and the uses to which music is now too often devoted! How many employ this gift to exalt self, instead of using it to glorify God! A love for music leads the unwary to unite with world lovers in pleasure gatherings where God has forbidden His children to go. Thus that which is a great blessing when rightly used, becomes one of the most successful agencies by which Satan allures the mind from duty and from the contemplation of eternal things. Music forms a part of God's worship in the courts above, and we should endeavor, in our songs of praise, to approach as nearly as possible to the harmony of the heavenly choirs.[11]

The price is far too high to turn our worship services into modern spiritual pep rallies that arouse and satisfy the flesh instead of subduing it. We should never allow this type of setting in the church, and thereby expose our young people to the influence and effects from the repetitious rhythms, lyrics, and simplistic melodies that are characteristic of modern Christian music. These features are conducive to inducing hypnotic phenomena. It is certainly good advice to break with questionable music styles and all forms of unrighteousness that

---

10   Ibid., p. 100.
11   Ellen G. White, *Patriarchs and Prophets*, p. 594.

so easily beset us and hinder our sanctification as well as our devotion to our Creator.

Chapter 18

Worship

When I go to the library and sit down in the reading room to study a subject, I am confronted with a notice that is on every table. The notice says SILENCE PLEASE. Why do you think that is there?

It is a well-known fact that when there is noise in the reading room the people who sit there will not be able to concentrate on what they are reading. The mind will be easily diverted, and thus it is a good rule to keep silence to prevent this.

Why do we go to church? To have a happy time listening to musicals and loud performances by a modern band, as if the church was a concert hall? Or do we go to church to pray and meet God, to worship and praise His holy name? Do we go to church to lift up our thoughts to our Creator with undisturbed devotion? If this is our purpose, then shouldn't there be silence around us? If we, as we may expect in church, like to hear God's voice speaking to our hearts, shouldn't there be a holy and quiet atmosphere?

Yes, the church is the place where God and angels are present to meet us as we assemble there. Even if there are only two or three gathered in His name, the promise is that God will be in their midst.[1] Will He be there only to be worshiped and praised? No, there is another very important objective. God wants to communicate with His worshiping children. How does He speak to those present in church?

The Bible tells us the story of Elijah. When threatened by Jezebel, he fled for his life and escaped eventually from her wrath to Horeb, the

---

1   Matt. 18:20

mountain of God, where he lodged in a cave.[2] Couldn't we in some way compare this mountain of God with the church, which is the house of God?

Horeb was a memorable holy place of communion where God communicated with Moses and with His people, proclaiming and giving them His holy law. This was the place where God met his servant Elijah and spoke to his heart. It is very important to learn the lesson of how God spoke to His servant.

We read that a strong wind came. The mountains were rent and the rocks broken. There was undoubtedly a lot of noise, but the Lord was not in the wind. After the wind there was an earthquake, but God was not in this impressive move either. Then there was a fire, another remarkable phenomenon, but again the Bible says that God was not in there.

Then, after the fire, there was a still small voice. When Elijah heard it he wrapped his face in his mantle. Why did he do that? It was a sign of reverence because of the presence of God.[3] In that still small voice God was present and He spoke to Elijah's heart.[4] The all-important fundamental lesson we should learn is that when we assemble in church to meet God there should not be a lot of noise. God's presence only goes together with reverential and peaceful quietness.

Jesus is our great example and He went to quiet, peaceful places to commune with His Father.[5] Jesus tells us, "But thou, when thou prayest, enter into thy closet, and when thou hast shut thy door, pray to thy Father which is in secret."[6] Thus, the place where we pray privately should be quiet with the door shut to secure undisturbed devotion. If we come to church to commune with God as a body of believers, there should be a similar peaceful and dedicated atmosphere, without any loud, exciting, and distracting phenomenon.

---

2   1 Kings 19:1–9
3   The angels veil their faces when they are in God's presence (Isa. 6:1, 2).
4   1 Kings 19:11–13
5   Matt. 14:23; Mark 1:35; 6:46; Luke 6:12
6   Matt. 6:6

The music in church should not be so loud as to drown and deafen the singing human voices. God is not in such loud music. God is not particularly worshiped by the mere sound of musical instruments. No, He is mainly worshiped by dedicated human voices. He will only truly be praised by grateful, humble human beings who have found comfort, peace, and salvation, by calling faithfully upon His holy name.

Chapter 19

Revival

We do not receive the rich blessing attached to the church service because its holy character has been lost. The church meeting has become more like a pleasant social gathering. In our worship to God, a revival and reformation needs to take place.

Ellen G. White writes:

> From the sacredness which was attached to the earthly sanctuary, Christians may learn how they should regard the place where the Lord meets with His people. There has been a great change, not for the better, but for the worse, in the habits and customs of the people in reference to religious worship. The precious, the sacred, things which connect us with God are far losing their hold upon our minds and hearts, and are being brought down to the level of common things. The reverence which the people had anciently for the sanctuary where they met with God in sacred service has largely passed away. Nevertheless, God Himself gave the order of His service, exalting it high above everything of a temporal nature.…
>
> Ardent, active piety should characterize the worshipers.
>
> If some have to wait a few minutes before the meeting begins, let them maintain a true spirit of devotion by silent meditation, keeping the heart uplifted to God in prayer …
> If when the people come into the house of worship, they have genuine reverence for the Lord and bear in mind that

they are in His presence, there will be a sweet eloquence in silence. The whispering and laughing and talking which might be without sin in a common business place should find no sanction in the house where God is worshiped....

The melody of song, poured forth from many hearts in clear, distinct utterance, is one of God's instrumentalities in the work of saving souls. All the service should be conducted with solemnity and awe, as if in the visible presence of the Master of assemblies....

It is too true that reverence for the house of God has become almost extinct.... Would it not be well for us often to read the directions given by God Himself to the Hebrews, that we who have the light of the glorious truth shining upon us may imitate their reverence for the house of God? We have abundant reason to maintain a fervent, devoted spirit in the worship of God. We have reason even to be more thoughtful and reverential in our worship than had the Jews. But an enemy has been at work to destroy our faith in the sacredness of Christian worship.[1]

We need a true perception of the holiness of God's church and its sacred services. We need a clear understanding of the required order, neatness, refined deportment, true reverence, and rightful worshipful frame of mind when we come into God's presence to receive the rich blessing that He has in store for us.

---

1   Ellen G. White, *Testimonies for the Church,* vol. 5, pp. 491–496.

Chapter 20

Praise

In the Bible we find clear instructions as to what kind of musical instruments were to be used for a holy purpose. The commandment of the Lord by His prophets was that the singing Levites for the service of the house of God were to use cymbals, psalteries and harps.[1]

The cymbal, a round, flat copper plate of about 10 to 15 cm in diameter, is not comparable to modern drums. Cymbals made a nice, clear tinkling sound and were used to signal the beginning of the song or a new stanza. Psalteries and harps are string instruments to accompany the singing. They do not produce dominant sounds that drown out the human voice.

At certain special services, such as the dedication of the temple, the great feasts, royal coronations, a joyful procession, or the cleansing of God's house in the days of King Hezekiah when great multitudes of people were present, the priests used their trumpets to play a part in the service:

> The trumpet was always used by the priests, and in the Divine service it was specially employed in calling the people together during the holy solemnities, and in drawing attention to new and successive parts of the ritual … The manner of blowing the trumpets was, first, by a long plain blast, then by one with breakings and quaverings, and then by a long plain blast again.[2]

---

1 2 Chron. 29:25; 2 Chron. 5:12, 13; 1 Chron. 25:6; 15:19–21
2 Robert Jamieson, A. R. Fausset, David Brown, *A Commentary Critical, Experimental and Practical on the Old and New Testaments*, vol. II, p. 518.

When multitudes of people were present at the various special services, those who stood far off would not hear the modest sound of the cymbal. To help people follow the succession of the service, the new parts were announced by the sound of the trumpet.

Some people argue that it could not be wrong to have loud music in church because the trumpet, which is a rather loud instrument, was also used in certain temple services. It should be clear however, that the trumpets had no musical function. "The trumpets of the priests constituted a separate body in every respect, with a ritual but not really musical function."[3]

We should understand that the real service of praise was by the human voice, while the modest sound of the prescribed string instruments only had a sustaining function. Alfred Edersheim, a Jewish convert to Christianity and doctor of Divinity at Oxford University, explains:

> Properly speaking, the real service of Praise in the Temple was only with the voice. This is often laid down as a principle by the rabbis. What instrumental music there was, served only to accompany and sustain the song … The melody was simple, sweet, and sung in unison to the accompaniment of instrumental music. Only one pair of brass cymbals were allowed to be used. But this 'sounding brass' and 'tinkling cymbal' formed no part of the Temple music itself, and served only as the signal to begin that part of the service … As already stated, the service of praise was mainly sustained by the human voice.[4]

Thus it is clear that there was no loud instrumental music in the Temple that accompanied the singing. People, who like loud music with drums in church, often refer to Bible passages translated as:

---

3   *Encyclopaedia Judaica*, vol. 12, p. 560.
4   Alfred Edersheim, *The Temple, Its Ministry and Services*, pp. 76, 78, 80.

"...play skilfully with a loud noise."[5]
"...make a loud noise, and rejoice, and sing praise."[6]

Lovers of loud music are particularly interested in these translations because they think it provides a biblical basis that supports their case nicely. If it would be proper to have a music band play in church, do these Bible passages justify us then to turn the amplifier's knobs high, as often happens, to produce as many decibels as possible? Is that in harmony with the real meaning of these Bible texts?

In the New Testament in Revelation 14:6–10 we meet three angels with a special message. It is stated that two of them are calling out their message with a *loud* voice. Does this mean that the purpose of their message is that it is to be proclaimed with many decibels? No, it rather means that this message is to be heralded with a clear and distinct voice, audibly to all people. So our worship and adoration of the only living true God does not mean that we should praise Him with many decibels, but rather that we should glorify, honor, and praise Him with a clear and distinct voice for He is the only one worthy to receive glory and honor.[7] Could these passages be translated otherwise with more exactness in their meaning?

Here are a few examples of other translations of these two passages. Note how the word 'loud' is either left out or related to the human voice:

"...strike up with all your art and shout in triumph."[8]
"...break into songs of joy, sing psalms."[9]
"...play skilfully, and shout for joy."[10]
"...burst into jubilant song with music."[11]

5   Ps. 33:3
6   Ps. 98:4
7   Rev. 4:11.
8   Ps. 33:3, NEB.
9   Ps. 98:4, NEB.
10   Ps. 33:3, NIV.
11   Ps. 98:4, NIV.

"…make the strings ring well!"[12]
"…break out and shout and make music."[13]

"…play skilfully with a joyful sound."[14]
"…break forth in joyful song; yes, sing praises!"[15]

"…play skilfully on the strings, with loud shouts."[16]
"…break forth into joyous song and sing praises."[17]

"…play skilfully with a beautiful rhythm."[18]
"…make ye merry and sing and give praise."[19]

We must keep in mind that there is not a perfect Bible translation. The King James Version is certainly a very good translation, but not completely perfect. We should always be very careful not to base our point of view on one or two translated words. The original Hebrew or Greek words used in the Bible may sometimes have different meanings, which make various translations possible. Before we jump to quick conclusions, it is always good to consult a dictionary or concordance, and compare different Bible translations.

Although the Bible clearly prescribes the kind of musical instruments that are to be used for sacred service in the temple, some people refer to Psalms 150, insisting that all kinds of musical instruments can be used in church, including drums, to praise God and to dance joyfully. They usually are very tenacious about this, thinking that they have a strong case, because the Psalm says, "Praise him with the timbrel and

---

12   Ps. 33:3, BY.
13   Ps. 98:4, BY.
14   Ps. 33:3, BV.
15   Ps. 98:4, BV.
16   Ps. 33:3, RSV.
17   Ps. 98:4, RSV.
18   Ps. 33:3, The Peshitta Bible, from ancient Eastern manuscripts.
19   Ps. 98:4, The Peshitta Bible, from ancient Eastern manuscripts.

dance."[20]

The timbrel, or tambourine, is a percussion instrument and its use in the temple was clearly prohibited. Is the Bible contradictory? If this is the case how are we to understand Psalm 150? Can this Psalm be understood as being God's prescription for the musical instruments to be used in the sacred temple services? Was this Psalm particularly directed to the Levites—the praise singers in the temple?

The last verse of this Psalm clearly says, "Let every thing that hath breath praise the Lord. Praise ye the Lord."[21] Thus it is unmistakable that this Psalm is not restricted to the Levites and the nation of Israel. No, praising God applies to every living being. Other Psalms also bear this clearly out, "O praise the Lord, all ye nations: praise him, all ye people."[22]

Does Psalm 150 in any way indicate that the temple was the only place where God could be praised? Are we perhaps to understand from this Psalm that everybody, armed with musical instruments including a timbrel, has to go up to the temple at Jerusalem to praise the Lord there?

If every living being—*everything that hath breath*—is supposed to praise the Lord, it is obvious that personal praise sessions at home, as well as public local religious praise activities are addressed. Most people would not be able to go up regularly to Jerusalem's temple and sing praises to the Lord there. We are not to suppose that praising the Lord would be restricted to only a few times a year, when at least the Hebrew people were supposed to attend the annual feasts. God bestows His children with many blessings, and there is sufficient reason to praise Him daily. Another Psalm says, "Seven times a day do I praise thee."[23] It is absolutely not imaginable that this manifold praising is meant to take place in the temple.

---

20   Ps. 150:4. The Hebrew word for "dance" is not quite clear and may have another meaning. The Berkeley Version, for instance, has the word "processional" and the King James Version has in the margin the word "pipe."
21   Ps. 150:6.
22   Ps. 117:1.
23   Ps. 119:164

If it is clear enough then that all personal and local public forms of praising the Lord are involved, then there is no contradiction or any problem as to the listed musical instruments, including the timbrel, since outside of the temple other musical instruments were allowed for common religious purposes and social activities.

Drum-like percussion instruments, such, as the timbrel, tabret, or tambourine, were not allowed to be used for sacred, divine worship, but were permitted for secular, daily life festival purposes. The timbrel, a rather small hand drum, was usually played by women[24] and used at special occasions, such as at a procession, weddings, or after victories over the enemy, when God is praised in thankful song and the timbrel provides the beat for a joyful dance or procession.[25]

The timbrel, tambourine, or tabret "was a typical women's instrument. It is mentioned seventeen times in the OT; thus it must have been very popular. Although it occurs in the Psalter and in religious hymns (Exod. 15; Jer. 31:4), it was not permitted in the temple. Its function in the Bible was restricted to secular or religious frolicking, cultic dances, or processions."[26]

There is no biblical support whatsoever that supports the use of drum-like instruments and loud electric guitars in church that drown out the human voice. The valid biblical principle is that music used for sacred church services should accompany the praise songs and not supplant the singing.

---

24   Ps. 68:25
25   Exod. 15:20, 21; see also 2 Sam. 6:5; 1 Chron. 13:8 when the ark was transported
26   *The Interpreter's Dictionary of the Bible,* vol. 3, p. 474.

Chapter 21

Hope

In spite of the many dangers that continuously threaten and surround us in the church in this modern age, there is hope! There is a special message calling people to worship the Creator of heaven and earth: the Three Angels Messages of Revelation 14.

If ever there was a time that this message is urgent and relevant, surely it is now. Fear God—Give glory to Him—Worship only Him who made all things—Don't walk in the ways of fallen Babylon—Don't join in with false worship.[1] Only the clear and pure message of the everlasting Gospel should be at the center of all of our church activities, instead of all kinds of human fabrications.

There should be no cherishing of modern forms of worship with contemporary music styles that pay homage to Satan and make people his prisoners. Rather, we are called to serve God and glorify Him only in all aspects of the Christian life.

Real hope for a true revival and a thorough reformation—a manifestation that God in this time of the end is waiting for in His church—can come only as we willingly and obediently listen to the prophet Jeremiah. He has the right and direct heavenly message from God for our modern age, "Thus saith the Lord, Stand ye in the ways, and see, and ask for the old paths, where is the good way, and walk therein, and ye shall find rest for your souls."[2]

May we by God's grace, walk in the old paths of the everlasting

---

1   Rev. 14:6–12
2   Jer. 6:16

gospel. May our praise and worship of the only true God, reflect the worship of heaven. Let us, who pretend to be God's final remnant, leave alone all the things that pertain to the broad and popular way that leads to destruction. Let us, who profess to serve the spotless Son of God, uphold the standards that match the narrow way that leads to everlasting life.[3] May God grant us the power to stay faithful watchmen on the walls of Zion, and to give the trumpet a clear and certain sound of warning in our time, which is undoubtedly the time of the end.

---

3   Matt. 7:13, 14

Bibliography

"The Mysteries of Music." Orthodox Advices. http://www.sfaturiorto-doxe.ro/orthodox/orthodox_advices_rock_music.htm.

"A Satanist Testifies About Rock." New Covenant Ministries. http://www.nccg.org/occult/Occult022-Rock2.html.

Baker, Paul. *Contemporary Christian Music, Where It Came From, What It Is, Where It's Going.* Westchester, IL: Crossway Books, 1985.

Barger, Erik. *From Rock to Rock: The Music of Darkness Exposed.* Lafayette, LA: Huntington House, 1990.

Beaujon, Andrew. *Body Piercing Saved My Life: Inside the Phenomenon of Christian Rock.* Boston, MA: Da Capo Press, 2006.

Blanchard, John, and Dan Lucarini. *Can We Rock the Gospel?* Webster, NY: Evangelical Press, 2006.

Boschman, LaMar. *The Rebirth of Music.* Bedford, TX: Revival Press, 1980.

Brothers, Fletcher, A. *The Rock Report: An 'Uncensored' Look into Today's Rock Music Scene.* Lancaster, PA: Starburst Publ., 1987.

Brown, Rebecca. *He Came to Set the Captives Free.* New Kensington, PA: Whitaker House, 1986.

Brown, Rebecca. *Prepare for War.* New Kensington, PA: Whitaker House, 1987.

Campbell, Don, ed. *Music: Physician for Times to Come.* 3rd ed. Wheaton, IL: Quest Books, 1995.

Cloud, David, W. *Contemporary Christian Music under the Spotlight.* Port Huron, MI: Way of Life, 1998.

Darsey, Steven. "John Wesley as Hymn and Tune Editor." *The Hymn: A Journal of Congregational Song.* Vol. 47. Richmond, VA: The Hymn Society, 1996.

Edersheim, Alfred. *The Temple, Its Ministry and Services.* Grand Rapids, MI: WM. B. Eerdmans Publishing Company, 1976.

Fisher, Tim. *The Battle for Christian Music.* Greenville, SC: Sacred Music Services, 2004.

Garlock, Frank, and Kurt Woetzel. *Music in the Balance.* Greenville, SC: Majesty Music, 1992.

Lafayette Girardeau, John. *Instrumental Music in Church Worship.* Dahlonega, GA: Crown Rights Book Comp, 2005, reprint.

Godwin, Jeff. *Dancing with Demons.* Chino, CA: Chick Publications, 1988.

Godwin, Jeff. *The Devil's Disciples, The Truth About Rock.* Chino, CA: Chick Publications, 1986.

Godwin, Jeff. *What's Wrong with Christian Rock?* Chino, CA: Chick Publications, 1990.

Gourley, Alan. *Assault on Childhood.* Sydney, Australia: First and Last Christian Publishing, 1988.

Hamel, Peter Michael. *Through Music to the Self.* Boulder, CO: Shambhala Publications, Inc., 1979.

Hart, Mickey, and Fredric Lieberman. *Planet Drum: A Celebration of Percussion and Rhythm.* San Francisco, CA: Harper, 1991.

Hart, Mickey, and Fredric Lieberman. *Spirit into Sound: The Magic of Music.* Novato, Petaluma, CA: Grateful Dead Books, Acid Test Productions, 1999, 2006.

Hart, Mickey, Jay Stevens, and Fredric Lieberman. *Drumming at the Edge of Magic: A Journey into the Spirit of Percussion.* San Francisco, CA: Harper, 1990.

Herman, Gary. *Rock 'n' Roll Babylon...* London: Plexus Publishing Ltd., 2002.

Jamieson, Robert, A. R. Fausset, and David Brown. *A Commentary Critical, Experimental and Practical on the Old and New Testaments.* Grand Rapids MI: Eerdmans, 1945.

Bryan Key, Wilson. *Media Sexploitation.* New York, NY: New American Library, 1976.

Bryan Key, Wilson. *Subliminal Seduction.* New York, NY: New American Library, 1981.

Lawhead, Steve. *Rock Reconsidered.* Downers Grove, IL: Inter Varsity Press, 1981.

Liemohn, Edwin. *The Chorale.* Philadelphia, PA: Muhlenberg Press, 1963.

Llewellyn, Ed. *The Truth About Subliminals.* St. Paul, MN: Llewellyn Publications, 1985.

Lucarini, Dan. *Why I left the Contemporary Christian Music Movement.* Webster, NY: Evangelical Press, 2007.

Makujina, John. *Measuring the Music.* PA: Old Paths Publications, 2002.

McElwain, Juanita. *The Lord is My Song.* Madison, TN: Print Quick, 2002.

Menconi, Al. *Should My Child Listen to Rock Music?* Elgin, IL: David C. Cook Publishing Co., 1991.

Miller, Steve. *The Contemporary Christian Music Debate, Worldly Compromise or Agent of Renewal?* Waynesboro, GA: OM Literature, 1993, 2007.

Morneau, Roger, J. *Beware of Angels.* Hagerstown, MD: Review and Herald Publishing Association, 1997.

Myers, Ivor. *Escape the Black Hole.* Nampa, ID: Pacific Press Publishing Association, 2007.

Neumann, Brian, S. *Van Rock en Roll tot Rots der Eeuwen.* Winterswijk, Netherlands: Inter Euro Publishing, 2005.

Osterman, Eurydice, V. *What God Says About Music.* Huntsville, AL: Awsahm Music, 1998.

Peters, Dan, Peters, Steve. *Rock's Hidden Persuader: The Truth about Back-masking.* Minneapolis, MN: Bethany House, 1985.

Peters, Dan, Steve Peters, and Cher Merrill. *What About Christian Rock?* Minneapolis, MN: Bethany House, 1986.

Piper, Keith. *Answers Book.* 5th ed. Sydney, Australia: Koorong Books, 2004.

Roth, Cecil, ed. *Encyclopaedia Judaica.* Jerusalem, Israel: Keter Publishing House Jerusalem Ltd., 1972.

Skinner, Quinton. *Casualties of Rock, (Behind the Music).* New York, NY: Pocket Books, Simon and Schuster, 2001.

Smith, Kimberly. *Let Those Who Have Ears to Hear.* Enumclaw, WA: Winepress, 2001.

Smith, Kimberly. *Music and Morals.* Enumclaw, WA: Winepress, 2005.

Spence, Hubert T. *Confronting Contemporary Christian Music.* Dunn, NC: 1997.

Than, Ker. *National Geographic News,* May 3, 2011.

Tame, David. *The Secret Power of Music.* Rochester, VA: Destiny Books, 1984.

The Interpreter's Dictionary of the Bible. Nashville, TN: Abingdon Press, 1980.

Tsatalbasidis, Karl. *Drums, Rock, and Worship.* Roseville, CA: Amazing Facts, 2003.

Valente, Mario. "The Liberation of Giani." *Review and Herald,* July 4, 1974.

Wade, T. E. *Spirit Possession.* Auburn, CA: Gazelle Publications, 1991.

Warren, Rick. *The Purpose Driven Church.* Grand Rapids, MI: Zondervan, 1995.

Warren, Rick. *The Purpose Driven Life.* Grand Rapids, MI: Zondervan, 2002.

Wenner, Jann, ed. Rolling Stone Magazine. February 12, 1976.

Wheaton, Jack. *Crisis in Christian Music.* Oklahoma City, OK: Hearthstone Publishing Ltd., 2000.

White, Charles. *The Life and Times of Little Richard*. New York, NY: Da Capo Press, 1984.

White, Ellen G. *The Early Elmshaven Years*. Vol. 5. Hagerstown, MD: Review and Herald Publishing Association, 1981.

White, Ellen G. *Early Writings*. Washington, DC: Review and Herald Publishing Association, 1882.

White, Ellen G. *The Great Controversy*. Mountain View, CA: Pacific Press Publishing Association, 1911.

White, Ellen G. *Medical Ministry*. Mountain View, CA: Pacific Press Publishing Association, 1932.

White, Ellen G. *Mind, Character, and Personality*. Vol. 1. Nashville, TN: Southern Publishing Association, 1977.

White, Ellen G. *Patriarchs and Prophets*. Washington, DC: Review and Herald Publishing Association, 1890.

White, Ellen G. *Selected Messages*. Book 2. Washington, DC: Review and Herald Publishing Association, 1958.

White, Ellen G. *The Story of Redemption*. Hagerstown, MD: Review and Herald Publishing Association, 1947.

White, Ellen G. *Testimonies for the Church*. Vol. 1. Mountain View, CA: Pacific Press Publishing Association, 1868.

White, Ellen G. *Testimonies for the Church*. Vol. 5. Mountain View, CA: Pacific Press Publishing Association, 1889.

White, Ellen G. *The Youth's Instructor*, October 26, 1899.

We invite you to view the complete
selection of titles we publish at:

www.TEACHServices.com

Scan with your mobile
device to go directly
to our website.

Please write or email us your praises, reactions, or
thoughts about this or any other book we publish at:

TEACH Services, Inc.
P U B L I S H I N G
www.TEACHServices.com ● (800) 367-1844

P.O. Box 954
Ringgold, GA 30736

info@TEACHServices.com

TEACH Services, Inc., titles may be purchased in bulk for
educational, business, fund-raising, or sales promotional use.
For information, please e-mail:

BulkSales@TEACHServices.com

Finally, if you are interested in seeing
your own book in print, please contact us at

publishing@TEACHServices.com

We would be happy to review your manuscript for free.

www.ingramcontent.com/pod-product-compliance
Lightning Source LLC
Chambersburg PA
CBHW060055100426
42742CB00014B/2837